CHURCHILL

ISBN 978-1-782811-49-7

Acknowledgements
The Imperial War Museum
Illustrated London News
Helen Wood

CHURCHILL

A PICTORIAL HISTORY OF HIS LIFE AND TIMES

TEXT BY

IAN S. WOOD

G2 entertainment

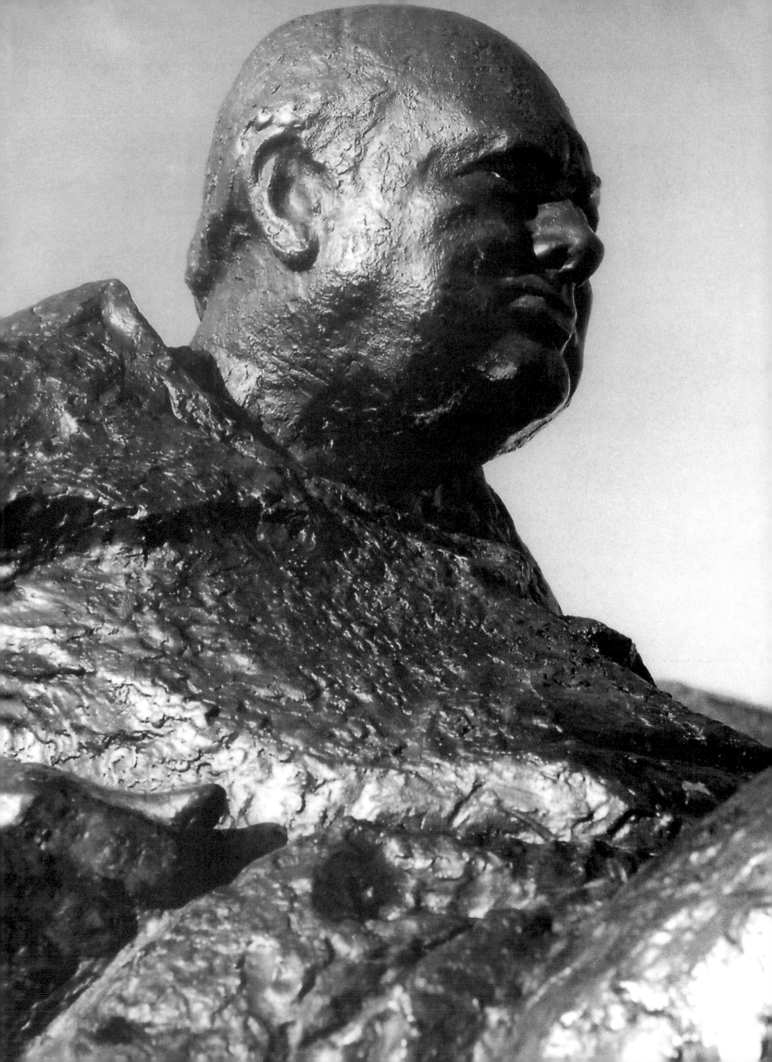

CONTENTS

CHAPTER 1
THE MAKING OF A STATESMAN
1874-1918

WINSTON LEONARD SPENCER CHURCHILL was a Victorian and an aristocrat. He was born on Saint Andrew's Day, 30 November 1874 in Blenheim Palace which was built at Woodstock, Oxfordshire, between the years 1705 and 1722. It was a monarch's reward to John Churchill, first Duke of Marlborough, for his victory over King Louis XIV's armies at Blenheim during the War of Spanish Succession in 1702. Church bells acclaimed the birth of a grandson to the 7th Duke. The baby's father was Lord Randolph, the Duke's younger son, who in 1874 had gained the Parliamentary seat of Woodstock for the Conservatives and

had also married the American heiress Jenny Jerome.

Since the time of the 1st Duke, the family's history had been a wayward one, notable for scandal and wild expenditure. Churchill's father lived extravagantly and his political career was volatile and ultimately self-destructive when he embarked on a rash trial of strength with the Prime Minister, the Marquess of Salisbury, over the budget he drew up in 1886 as Chancellor of the Exchequer. As a child, the young Winston longed for the affection of parents too often absent and found a substitute for it from Mrs Everest, his nurse. She died

left: Churchill aged 7, 1881.

in 1894 and he later described her as 'my dearest and most intimate friend during the whole of the twenty years I had lived.' Schooling also separated him from his parents, first at a sadistic preparatory establishment from which Mrs Everest was instrumental in having him removed, and ultimately at Harrow, which he attended from April 1888 until 1892. His record there was undistinguished though he enjoyed history and English literature, but he needed special tuition in mathematics to pass the 1893 entrance examination for Sandhurst Military Academy. He was happier there than he had been at school and in 1895 was commissioned as an officer in the 4th Hussars, a very fashionable cavalry regiment whose social style and mess bills became an immediate problem for his mother, who had been widowed the previous year.

She may have been in financial difficulties but she spared none of her personal and political influence to further her son's military career. This initially took him to India with his regiment but he had little liking for the expatriate British community he found there. In a letter home he wrote of some of the women he saw at the races. 'Nasty, vulgar creatures all, looking as though they thought themselves great beauties. I fear they are all a sorry lot.' Apart from his military duties and playing polo, he spent his time furthering his education with books sent out by his mother. He also found what he most wanted, real action on the North-West frontier.

This frontier's proximity to Afghanistan and the fear of dissident tribes linking up with Russian agents

right: Churchill as subaltern in full dress uniform of the 4th Queen's Own Hussars, 1895.

above: Rudyard Kipling, novelist, playwright and poet.

made the area one of Britain's strategic priorities. Churchill quickly learned his trade there in vicious close combat of a kind immortalised in Kipling's lines:

'When you're wounded and left
on Afghanistan's plains
An' the women come out to
cut up what remains
Jest roll to your rifle an' blow
out your brains
An' go to your Gawd like a
soldier'

Churchill's detractors have always claimed that he liked war. He certainly wrote about it graphically in letters home, in books like *The Story of the Malakand Field Force,* published in 1898 and *The River War,* on his time serving under Kitchener in the Sudan, and also articles for the Morning Post from South Africa. He never, however, condoned brutality for its own sake, writing to his mother that in the 1898 victory of Omdurman in which he charged with the British cavalry 'was disgraced by the inhuman slaughter of the wounded and that Kitchener was responsible for this.'

His South African exploits as a reporter, participant in some major military action and escaping from a Boer prison camp, earned him celebrity status as well as a seat in Parliament which he won as Conservative and Unionist candidate in Oldham in the general Election of October 1900. The British Empire and the self-promotion which it, along with his own energy and courage, made possible, had got him there and his belief in Britain's imperial destiny had been confirmed by his own experiences. This was echoed in his early speeches but he was never drawn to Joseph Chamberlain's espousal of the cause of tariff reform as a way to bind the Empire closer through preferential trading relationships within it. He castigated Chamberlain's case as 'a greedy gospel of materialism and expediency' unworthy of the high ideals of Empire and in May 1904 crossed the floor of Parliament to join the Liberals who denounced tariff reform as a scheme which would drive up the cost of living in Britain.

Temperamentally, it has been argued, Churchill may not have been a team player in the party game but for the next ten years he gave all of his energies to the Liberal cause. The party's constituency organisation in Manchester North West adopted him as their candidate for the General Election of 1906 in which the Conservatives were routed and he received his first ministerial appointment in the new government. This was as Parliamentary Under-Secretary for the Colonies and he quickly found himself actively involved in making a reality of the case for reconciliation with the defeated Boers in South Africa which he had already made eloquently from the Opposition benches in the Commons. An early memorandum to his minister, Lord Elgin, has been called 'a classic statement of the primary principle of political conduct of the Victorian and Edwardian elite, the principle of timely concession to retain an ultimate control'

This was true in the sense that Churchill's policy helped to give the Boers the substance of selfgovernment within the union of South Africa. Racial apartheid would later be ruthlessly applied by the state's Boer or Afrikaner rulers but African rights had little place in the debates of 1906 and 1907 nor, it must be said, did they loom large in

right: Churchill in 1900.

Churchill's fairly paternalist priorities at that time. This is ironical given that a young Nelson Mandela greatly admired his defiant Second World War broadcasts from London.

Churchill's energetic work at the Colonial Office earned him a Cabinet appointment as President of the Board in Trade in April 1908. Constitutional convention then required that newly-appointed ministers re-contest their seats in Parliament. Churchill did so and lost in Manchester but was quickly adopted for a vacant Dundee seat by the Liberal association there. He knew little of and never learned much about Scotland but Dundee, or 'Juteopolis' as it was often called because of its dominant industry and the huge workforce it employed in atrocious conditions, kept him in Parliament for the next fourteen years.

right: Churchill, on the right, taken prisoner by the Boers.

One link Churchill did forge with Scotland was through his marriage that same year to Clementine Hozier. Her father, the Earl of Airlie and her mother separated when she was only six. Her upbringing and education were thus a product of 'reduced circumstances' and there was no question of Churchill seeking her as a 'good match' This may have been one reason among many for the enduring success of a marriage in which Clementine not only gave him five children, though one died very young, but often forcefully expressed opinions on political issues and personalities. Their relationship survived many separations brought about by Churchill's political career but as time went on, she came to play an increasingly public role. He refers to her only in the final sentence of his memoir *My Early Life* when he writes of 'September 1908, when I married and lived happily ever afterwards.'

The Board of Trade was a department with a major role in a broadening Liberal programme of social reform. Churchill espoused this programme with eloquence and energy, pushing through legislation to protect workers in 'sweated trades' and setting up labour exchanges to help the unemployed find work. His conception of state welfare was never a universalist one: he saw the state's role as being to provide a safety net to help working class families escape the worst results of joblessness and low pay. He took an interest in German welfare polices and in 1908 made what has been called a 'Bismarckian' case to the Prime minister, Asquith, for National insurance legislation, a modernised Poor Law, expanded state schooling and an active state role in industry. 'Germany' he argued, 'is

left: Ladysmith camp. British troops in active service in the Transvaal, 1899.

below: 20 pounder Boer gun at Mafeking, 1900.

organised not only for war, but for peace. We are are organised for nothing except party politics.'

Churchill was a loyal lieutenant to David Lloyd George in the drama unleashed in 1909 by the People's Budget' which raised death duties, land value taxation and income tax as well as calling for a supertax' on exceptionally high incomes. He was attacked with fury by his own class, especially when he supported House of Lords reform to stop the upper chamber from blocking the budget, as the Tory peers tried to do, and limiting their delaying power over other legislation. This confrontation forced two General Elections in 1910, Churchill remaining at centre stage though appointed Home Secretary in February of that year. In this new office, he backed humane prison reforms and recommended reprieves by the Crown in nearly half of the cases which came to him involving death sentences, but drew heavy fire for endorsing the forced feeding of suffragette prisoners on hunger strike. This was a degrading business though the alternative was to let them die.

Churchill gave qualified support to their cause but was an uncompromising opponent of their militancy and law-breaking, as indeed he was of some of the tactics used by trade unionists in the wave of strikes which swept British industry in the period before 1914. His reaction to events in the South Wales coalfield where he authorised the use of troops in support of police, notably in the town of Tonypandy, would haunt him for years. There had been a brief out-break of looting there but the army's presence caused no fatalities. Three strikers were shot dead the following

left: Field Marshal Lord Kitchener, photographed in 1916.

year during the bitter railway and dock disputes in Wales and in Liverpool and many blamed Churchill though he was in fact an advocate of legal rights for trade unions and in 1908 had received a hero's welcome in South Wales because of his support for the Liberal government's eight hour day legislation for miners.

Churchill's temperament drew him to crisis and confrontation like a moth to a flame and this was typified by his urge to be present in person at Sidney Street, East London early in 1911. This was when gunmen, thought to be East European anarchists who had shot and killed three policemen, barricaded themselves in a house and exchanged fire with guardsmen brought in at Churchill's instigation to support the police.

This image of himself as a man of action made his next ministerial appointment seem a dream fulfilled. In October 1911, Asquith asked him to become First Lord of the Admiralty. This meant, in a darkening international situation, taking day-to-day responsibility for the world's mightiest navy. Churchill immersed himself in this task, managing before the outbreak of war to spend a total of eight months at sea on every type of ship, learning at first hand the needs and priorities of the senior service.

These were years of turbulence as the crisis over Irish Home Rule and resistance to it by Unionist Ireland and Loyalist Ulster tested to breaking point the will of Churchill's ministerial colleagues. He was accused by unionists of betraying his father's memory when he supported a firm stance by the cabinet. 'My personal view' he later wrote, 'had always been that I would never coerce Ulster to make her come under a

right: Suffragette prisoner on a hunger strike being force-fed by prison authorities, 1912.

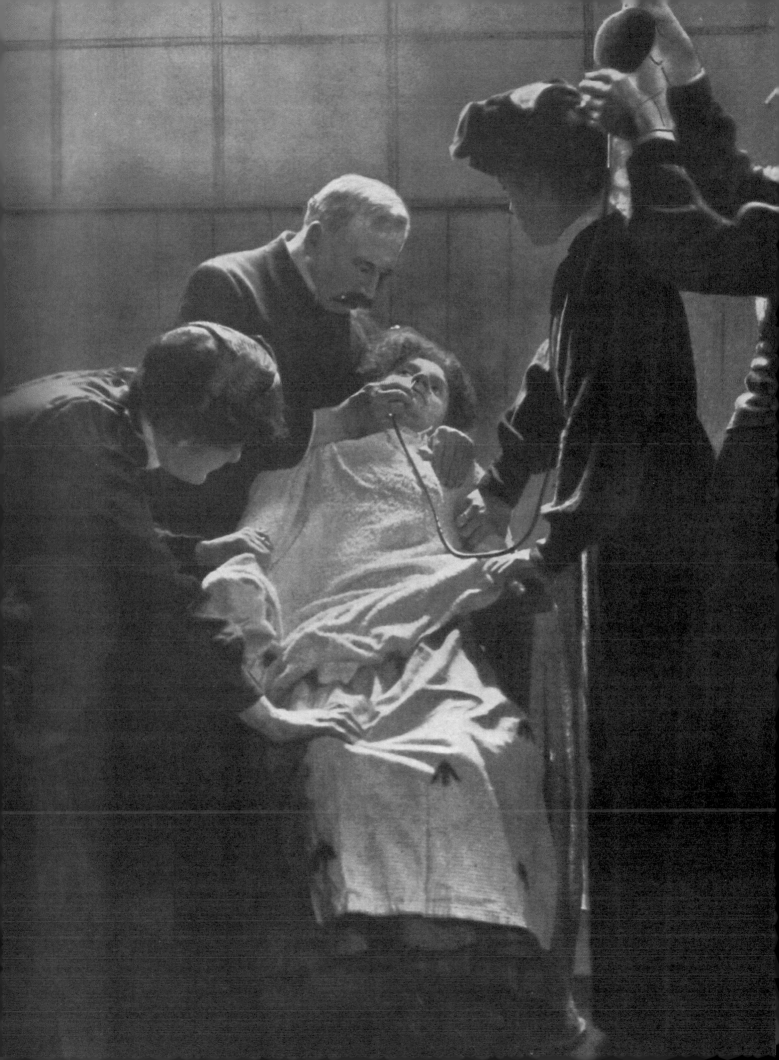

above: In 1911 two foreign anarchists kept over 1,000 police and military at bay in Sidney Street, London. Here a marksman on a ladder looks out.

Dublin government but that I would do all that was necessary to prevent her stopping the rest of Ireland having the Parliament they desired.' As prospects of any compromise receded, Churchill acted in March 1914, ordering the navy's Fifth Battle Squadron to take station off the Isle of Arran in the Clyde, no great sailing distance from Belfast Lough in case of armed action by opponents of Home Rule.

This was long remembered by Ulster Loyalists but in fact the Liberal government, fearful of a worsening situation in Europe, backed off from military action and when war came in 1914, its Home Rule legislation was put on hold. By then the navy was ready though Churchill had not achieved the increases in expenditure he had demanded from exasperated colleagues who recalled his support for reduced naval estimates before he

became First Lord. On 1 August 1914, two full days before Britain's declaration of war, he ordered full mobilisation of the fleet without reference to the cabinet which merely confirmed it the next day.

Typically, with the war only two months old, Churchill, in a bizarre communiqué to Asquith, offered on 5 October, to resign from the Cabinet in order to assume command of the defence of Antwerp where Belgian and British forces were under heavy pressure from the advancing Germans. In due course the port fell, but Churchill was right about its strategic importance and his flamboyant intervention may have helped it hold out longer.

It was not Antwerp but the Dardanelles which came close to destroying Churchill's career. the period of his direct responsibility for operations there was brief and ended for all practical purposes when naval attacks on Turkish forts in the Straits were called off on 18 march 1915. At the start of the year, Churchill was under criticism for the navy could claim only one victorious surface action off the Falklands and his relations with the admirals were tense. His most important ally was the First Sea Lord, Jackie Fisher, a choleric and, Churchill came to believe, an unstable character twenty years his senior, who initially supported the concept of naval action to force a passage through the Straits in order to open up a new front against Germany's ally. Fisher, however, joined the doubters in the Cabinet once it became clear in his own mind that Churchill believed warships could do the job without substantial ground forces landing on the Turkish shore.

When troop landings were decided on, Churchill supported them but had little control over the catastrophic way these were conducted. The awful loss-rate among the units who landed on the Gallipoli peninsula in April 1915 created a deathless legend, especially in Australia and New Zealand but they were coincidental with the collapse of Churchill's relationship with Fisher, who resigned on 15 May. This sealed Churchill's fate as Asquith planned to form a coalition government in which, with Fisher gone, he would be unable to keep Churchill at the Admiralty.

Churchill was demoted to the Chancellorship of the Duchy of Lancaster. He accepted though his wife feared what the mental effect on him might be and Max Aitken, Conservative MP and newspaper

right: Mr & Mrs Churchill at Hendon Aerodrome, 1914.

magnate soon to be Lord Beaverbrook, wrote of him at this time as a 'lost soul'. Churchill resigned from the government in November 1915 and soon afterwards accepted the command of a Scottish infantry battalion in France, a role in which his performance was eccentric but also courageous and effective.

Churchill never retreated from his belief in the strategic case for the Dardanelles campaign and devoted much of *The World Crisis,* his history of the war and its aftermath, to restating it. It may be however, that he willed the end, a second front in the Near East to defeat Turkey and rejuvenate Russia as an ally, without addressing the logistic means to its attainment. This was a charge made against him in the Second World War too but in 1915 the inter-service co-operation needed for operations such as those attempted in the Dardanelles was in its infancy. Churchill, moreover, had no responsibility for command failures on the ground, though in fact the allied troops came close at times to breaking out of the grim terrain of the Gallipoli peninsula. Only when the Dardanelles committee published its first report in March 1917, assigning as much blame to Kitchener and Asquith as to Churchill did his return from the wilderness begin to be possible.

The new Prime Minister, Lloyd George, had prepared the ground with care before bringing him back to office as Minister of Munitions. This decision got a hostile press and a furious Conservative reaction but Churchill threw all his energies into his new appointment and relished the opportunities it gave him to visit the

top left: A wiring party of guardsmen crossing a captured canal on 1917.
below left: British Front in Flanders, 1917.

above: David Lloyd George.

above: Churchill and Clementine, Armistice day, 11 November 1918.

Western Front. His alternative 'Eastern Strategy' may have collapsed the previous year at the Dardanelles, but the cost of British offensives in the West appalled him. 'Never for a moment,' he wrote to his wife in May 1917, 'does the thought of this carnage and ruin escape my mind' and later that year he strongly opposed Haig's Third Ypres attack. Haig, the British Commander-in-Chief, in turn, began to suspect Churchill as a meddler plotting against him. Churchill, for his part, came close to despair at the weakness of a government unable to dismiss commanders in the field in whom they no longer had confidence. This was something that he would not flinch from as Prime Minister in a later conflict.

left: Crowds celebrate Armistice Day outside Buckingham Palace. The Royal Family watch from the balcony, 1918.

CHAPTER 2

POWER AND ISOLATION

1918-1939

AFTER HIS COALITION government's General Election victory in December 1918. Lloyd George made Churchill his Secretary of State for War but began to regret doing so when it became clear to him that their views were wholly different on the role of the 200,000 British and allied troops still in Russia. On 31 December, the Cabinet agreed that these forces should not take sides in the vicious civil war which had started between the new Bolshevik state and its enemies. Churchill's hatred of the Bolsheviks and his vivid fears of the threat they posed to democratic states and to the British Empire made it impossible for him to accept this. On the issue, he succeeded only in isolating himself within the coalition government, exasperating Lloyd George, an old ally, and alarming both the service chiefs and a war-weary public by the way he took his advocacy of what could only have been a hazardous military venture out of the Cabinet and to the press and public platforms.

As big a preoccupation for Churchill in his new ministry was Ireland, where dramatic changes had taken place since 1914. The

left: Churchill at Epping during the declaration of the poll, November 1935.

constitutional Nationalist party was routed by Sinn Fein in the 1918 election and co-ordinated attacks against Crown forces were started early the following year by IRA units who felt they were carrying on the fight begun by the men and women of the ill-fated Easter rising of 1916. Churchill saw the army's role as backing up the Royal Irish Constabulary (RIC) who along with hastily raised auxiliary units of ex-soldiers had to confront the IRA threat. It took time for Churchill to see the political dangers of increasingly ruthless tactics against the IRA and its real or imagined supporters, despite appeals to him by his wife to be wary of what she called 'iron-fisted Hunnish' methods.

He also, however, supported political initiatives like the 1920 Government of Ireland Act, setting up a Parliament and devolved administration in the North; similar provision for the rest of Ireland was ignored by the republican leadership. Partition became a reality accompanied by appalling sectarian violence in the new Northern state and Churchill, who was moved to the Colonial Office in February 1921, came out in support of Lloyd George's view that a truce in Ireland might be possible. This finally came in July and Churchill was appointed one of the British negotiators in the complex talks which led to the Anglo-Irish Treaty signed in December. The outcome Churchill favoured was dominion status for any new Irish state with continued allegiance to the Crown. Michael Collins, one of the Irish negotiators who had achieved some personal rapport with Churchill, had fought for an all-Ireland republic but signed the treaty as a tactical necessity, knowing his

above: The Lille Victory Parade, November 1918, is watched by Lieutenant-Colonel Montgomery, behind whom is Churchill, Minister of Munitions.

life could be taken in the IRA split which would result.

Churchill has been accorded his share of credit for the achievement of the treaty though there are those who argue that he would have supported all-out war against the IRA if its leaders had rejected it or if the anti-Treaty side had prevailed in the Irish civil war which followed. His contribution to the 1920-21 Irish 'settlement' was driven very much by his perception of British interests like the guarantee accepted by the new Irish state of the Royal Navy's continued access to ports under its jurisdiction. He would later react with fury when Eamon de Valera's government abrogated the relevant clauses of the treaty in preparation for its policy of neutrality in the Second World War.

As Colonial Secretary, Churchill had concerns which went far beyond what he famously described as 'the dreary steeples of Fermanagh and Tyrone'. He had strong Zionist sympathies and had long supported the case for a Jewish 'national home' in Palestine. As a minister his commitment to this remained, though he put his name, in June 1922, to a White Paper which stressed that not all Palestine could become a Jewish state and that Jewish settlement would not be allowed to subordinate Arabs or their religion and culture. British interests in the Middle East, he felt, could be secured as much through control of territories 'mandated' to it by the new League of Nations, like Transjordan and Iraq, as by using Jewish settlement as an instrument of policy.

Churchill's imperialism, for which he has been much vilified, was of its time in its attitudes but was not inhumane. In July 1920, while still

right: Deutschmarks doubling as children's building bricks, Germany, 1923, during the chronic post-war inflation.

above: King George V, 1929.

left: Ramsey Macdonald, British politician who became first Labour PM in 1924.

Secretary of State for War, he eloquently supported disciplinary action against General Richard Dyer for causing more than 400 deaths by ordering troops to open fire on a nationalist demonstration at Amritsar in India, while over Iraq, he clashed with Sir Hugh Trenchard, Chief of the Air Staff, over loss of life among tribal dissidents caused by the new RAF in its 'air policing' role.

Churchill's four postwar years in ministerial office were accompanied both by personal tragedy and also new happiness for him and Clementine. Their youngest daughter, Marigold, fell sick and died in August 1921, aged only three and a half, but the following year Clementine gave birth safely to another daughter, who would become Lady Mary Soames. In this year he also bought Chartwell in Kent. Now maintained by the National Trust, it remains uniquely Churchill's creation, largely rebuilt and landscaped by him. It became his weekend and holiday refuge where he could entertain, write, paint or dig and lay bricks as the humour took him. One structure that always attracts visitors is 'Marycot', a brick playhouse he built for his new daughter and her friends. The sign he designed for it, 'Children Only', remains in place to this day.

The November 1922 General Election which unseated Churchill gave the Conservatives an overall majority in Parliament but a year later Stanley Baldwin, who had taken over as Prime Minister from the

left: **The General Strike**. Guardsmen return from Hackney and the London docks at the General Strike, 1926.

During the General Strike, Churchill, although opposed to it, supported the miners' call for a national minimum wage. His cabinet colleagues disapproved of his involvement and his attempt at reconciliation was rejected.

above: Joseph Stalin, right with Lenin, founder of the USSR, 1922.

'Churchill is the kind of man who will pick your pocket of a kopeck if you don't watch him.' This was Stalin's verdict on Churchill, two years after they first met in Moscow in August 1942. Churchill had in his early years been a bitter opponent of the Soviet state created by Lenin. Their relationship, a product of their need for each other as allies, against Hitler, alternated between mutual suspicion and hard-drinking bonhomie.

terminally ill Andrew Bonar Law, asked for a dissolution of Parliament to fight a new election on the case for protective import duties as the best answer to growing unemployment. His decision brought Labour to office for the first time as a minority government and enabled Churchill to stand for the last time as a Liberal. This was in West Leicester where on a programme of Free Trade and anti-Socialism he lost again to Labour.

Churchill's anti-Socialism, fuelled by his continuing fear of Bolshevism, was drawing him back to the Conservative fold though he continued to believe in active state policies to extend social reform. Three months into the lifetime of the Labour government, he stood again at a by-election in the Abbey Division of Westminster. This time he campaigned as an 'Independent Anti-Socialist' and lost by only forty three votes to the official Conservative

candidate. The Liberal vote in this contest collapsed and by May 1924, Churchill was in Liverpool addressing Conservative audiences once more. In September, the safely Conservative Epping constituency adopted him as a 'Constitutional' candidate. Labour fell from power the following month and in the ensuing General Election, dominated as it was by strident talk of Soviet-backed subversion in Britain, Churchill was in his element. He returned to Parliament with a 10,000 majority and was soon afterwards formally re-admitted to the Conservative Party.

He was also, much to his surprise, asked to join Baldwin's Cabinet. Some writers have argued this was a result of the Prime Minister's premonitions of trouble if he excluded Churchill, whose surprise was compounded by the offer of the Chancellorship of the Exchequer, the very office his father had held forty years earlier under Lord Salisbury. Churchill threw himself with typical energy into his work as Chancellor and embarked almost at once upon a confrontation with his old department, the Admiralty. 'That extraordinary fellow Winston has gone mad,' wrote Admiral Beatty, the First Sea Lord, in 1925, 'economically mad, and no sacrifice is too great to achieve what in his short-sightedness is the panacea for all evil – to take a shilling off the Income Tax.' If naval building had to be cut back to bring public expenditure under control Churchill was ready to do it just as he was ready to take Britain back on to the Gold Standard.

The First World War had badly shaken the world's money markets and legislation soon after it suspended the Gold Standard – the fixed price at which gold traded in major currencies – for a six year period. Churchill accepted the traditional view of the Gold Standard as essential to stable currencies and expanding trade. He took the risk that a return to gold might push up the bank rate, thus adversely affecting investment and exports. The Bank of England and Treasury view upon which he acted had more upholders than critics at the time, with the exception of the great economist John Maynard Keynes. Churchill later admitted his decision had been a mistake and it deepened the crisis in a coal industry riven by conflict which culminated in the General Strike of 1926.

The call for a General Strike by the General Council of the Trades Union Congress in May 1926, was an act of solidarity with miners in bitter

right: Admiral Sir David Beatty, Commander-in-Chief of the British Fleet, 1918.

dispute with the coal companies. Churchill was for a long time represented by the Labour movement and the left as having taken a consistently hard line over the strike, but his view of it was little different from Baldwin's. He, like Churchill, saw it as an unconstitutional act and trusted his Chancellor to put the government's case robustly in the British Gazette. Churchill's position was always that two disputes were at issue. One was the unconstitutional challenge of the General Strike which had to be defeated and indeed was, after only nine days. The other was the coal strike which dragged on for many months. His attitude was much more flexible about this, though at times he resorted to the language of threat and coercion. Sir Martin Gilbert, his official biographer, reveals to us a Churchill ready to isolate himself within the Cabinet over his urging of the case for an agreement covering the whole industry under which owners would be compelled to make substantial concessions.

This may have been Churchill the one-nation paternalist talking but some of his words and actions made it difficult for him to shake off the hard line image created by his earlier role as Home Secretary during a period of major strikes and he still saw the hand of Soviet Bolshevism behind most industrial unrest. Well ahead of the General Strike, he had fully supported the government's decision to have the leaders of Britain's small Communist party arrested and imprisoned. Throughout the remainder of the Baldwin government, however, he supported increased funding for old age and widows'

left: Stanley Baldwin, who was three times Prime Minister in the inter-war years.

pensions and legislation to dismantle what was left of the often punitive nineteenth century Poor Law.

With the defeat of the Conservatives in the May 1929 General Election. other preoccupations intervened as Churchill returned to the back benches in Parliament where he would remain until the outbreak of the Second World War. Sir Martin Gilbert called this period 'the wilderness years', a term that fits the frustrations of his subject's exclusion from the influence he craved on policy decisions vital to Britain's role in Europe and beyond. Loss of office reduced Churchill's salary to that of an ordinary member of the Commons but his lifestyle of travel and entertaining was costly and a strain on his finances. The Wall Street crash of 1929, which he witnessed while in America that October, caused him heavy losses. On his return, his daughter Mary later recalled, Chartwell was run down to a low ebb: 'the big house was dust sheeted, only the study being left open.'

A bleak period followed of life in London hotels and short-let houses, until a lucrative lecture tour of the United States over the winter of 1931-32. which brought Churchill contracts from American publishers and newspapers. This, along with good investment advice, assisted the restoration of his finances but his work rate as author and journalist was an extraordinary one. Between October 1933 and September 1938 he completed the four-volume life of his great ancestor, the 1st Duke of Marlborough and began work on his 'History of the English-Speaking Peoples' though this was only

above: Edward VIII and his three brothers. From left to right – the Duke of Kent, Edward VIII, the Duke of York and the Duke of Gloucester.

published after the Second World War. One of his private secretaries later told of how on occasions she would mount a ladder at Chartwell to take dictation from Churchill while he was bricklaying!

The two issues which consumed his energies in the decade before his return to ministerial office in September 1939 were the political and constitutional future of India and what Britain's response should be to the predatory and aggressive demands of Hitler after he took power in Germany early in 1933. On India, his rejection of Conservative policy may have isolated him politically, weakened the influence he hoped to have on policy towards Hitler and a rearmed Germany and reinforced his reputation for impetuosity. There can, however, be no doubting his belief in Britain's imperial role in

India and the danger of constitutional change. In 1930 Churchill famously described India in a speech as 'the jewel in the imperial crown' yet he had shown no inclination to revisit it since his army service there more than thirty years before and had been highly critical of the British expatriate community he had encountered. His angry repudiation of Conservative policy on India was rooted in his unease over the coalition government's 1917-19 reforms which had conceded India some nominal self-government, albeit not enough to satisfy Gandhi's increasingly militant Congress movement. When in 1929 Baldwin, as Conservative leader, came close to accepting the Labour government's case for negotiated Dominion status for India, Churchill was appalled. In January 1931, he resigned from the

left: Gandhi arriving at 10 Downing Street for a meeting with Ramsey Macdonald in 1931.

The rise of the Nazis. above: Hitler opening the Berlin Olympics, 8 August 1936.

right, top: Dr Joseph Goebbels, Nazi Minister of Propaganda, pictured here, in 1934 at a demonstration at the Saar frontier.

right, below: Hitler receives a welcome as he enters Sudetenland, 1938.

In 1932, on a rare visit to Germany, Churchill lost a chance to meet Hitler. His declared aversion to anti-semitism was a major reason for this. Even then, he had an instinctive sense of the evil the Nazis could unleash in Germany and beyond, once they had power.

Opposition front bench in Parliament to rally support 'for British rights and British interests in India, for two centuries of effort and achievement, lives given on a hundred fields, for more lives given and consumed in faithful and devoted service to the Indian people themselves.'

The chance for Churchill to block government intentions on India came in the 1934-35 session of Parliament when Sir Samuel Hoare, Secretary of State for India, introduced hugely complex legislation designed to set up an all-India federation with its own two-chamber legislative body to bring together the provinces and the princely states. A nucleus of sixty Conservative backbenchers supported Churchill's impassioned attacks on this bill but he turned increasingly to the party's

constituency activists in speeches brilliant in content and delivery but apocalyptic in their predictions of doom if the National Government had its way. Despite Churchill's sustained rhetoric, the India Bill became law in 1935. It failed to resolve the sub-continent's problems and Churchill's intemperate language, especially about Gandhi and his Congress movement, brought him new enemies while alienating potential allies from the Conservative party's reformist and socially progressive wing who came to agree with his foreign policy views.

These views and the way Churchill developed them into a powerful and passionate critique of British policy towards Nazi Germany define for many people the history of the 1930s, a 'low, dishonest decade' as the poet W H Auden called it, in

right: Gandhi walking past British soldiers.

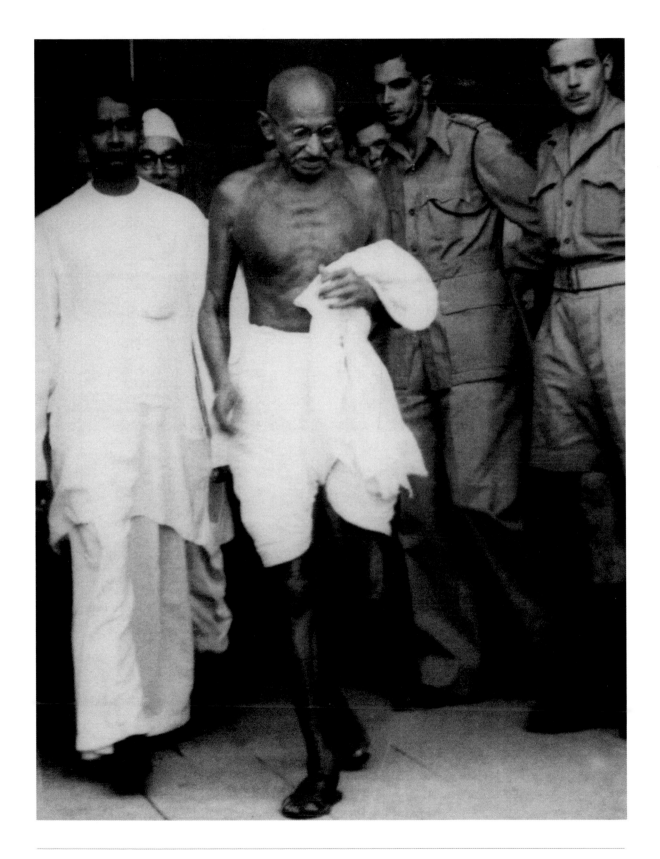

above top and above: Chamberlain at Munich, 1938.

above: The Four Powers Conference, Munich 30 September 1938.
Seen here are, left to right, Field Marshal Göring, Benito Mussolini,
Hitler and Count Ciano, the Italian Foreign Minister.

which liberal democracies like France and Britain were infirm of purpose in their response to aggressive Fascism. Nobody did more than Churchill, in speeches and in his hugely successful history of the Second World War, published between 1948 and 1954, to vilify and demonise the word appeasement as a way of describing the belief that renewed war could be avoided by compromises with and concessions to dictators. Appeasement and the concept it stood for, of avoiding war by negotiation and rational bargaining were not new ideas, but Churchill's eloquence froze both into a context of condemnation from which it has been impossible to prise them even sixty years later.

Churchill never met Hitler and only twice visited Germany over a thirty year period before 1939 yet, in an almost intuitive way, he sensed the malign potential of the Nazi regime. Even so, he moved with caution in challenging National Government policy. Despite repeated acts of aggression by Mussolini and Hitler and despite his doubts about the adequacy of Britain's rate of rearmament, Churchill never cast a vote against the National Government until after the September 1938 Munich Agreement which allowed the dismemberment of democratic Czechoslovakia on Hitler's terms.

He did not perceive as a personal attack on Chamberlain his biting criticism of the agreement in Parliament on 5 October, when he declared that 'the German dictator, instead of snatching the victuals from the table, has been content to have them served to him course by course.' Indeed the previous year, he had seconded Chamberlain's nomination at the Conservative conference to succeed Baldwin as party leader. Churchill's dilemma was that while feeling the deepest unease about government policy, he also wanted to be back in office in order to influence and redirect it. However, his decision, along with just 29 colleagues, to abstain on the Munich vote, brought him no closer to office. His correspondence in the ensuing weeks reveal a sense of isolation: he was not rewarded for his Munich speech nor for his abstention in Parliament with the deluge of congratulatory mail which greeted Chamberlain on his return from Munich.

Elements within his own Epping constituency party moved unsuccessfully to stop Churchill's re-adoption as their election candidate. They saw his Munich speech as disloyalty while those who shared his doubts looked more to Anthony Eden as a potential leader. For them, Churchill was still a volatile and impetuous figure who, after all, only two years previously had gone out on a limb politically to give abortive support to Edward VIII in the Abdication crisis. However, when Churchill finally did vote against the Government, on 17 November 1938, on the issue of creating a new Ministry of Supply, Chamberlain was already having doubts about the continuing popularity of appeasement. By the spring of 1939, even before Hitler's invasion of Czechoslovakia, in a brutal and, Churchill argued, predictable violation of the Munich terms, public opinion was starting to move away from Chamberlain and towards Churchill. When war came, on 3 September, the Prime Minister had little option but to include his foremost critic in a restructured government.

CHAPTER 3

'WINSTON IS BACK'

THE PHONEY WAR
SEPTEMBER 1939 – MAY 1940

WHETHER THE SIGNAL 'Winston is back' was ever in fact sent out by the Admiralty to British ships when Churchill returned to office, as its First Lord on September 1939, has never been substantiated. Even so, his return to the same position he had held at the outbreak of a previous war must have had an effect on naval officers with any sense of their service's history. Indeed, those old enough to remember Churchill's robust and interventionist style as First Lord, may well have had premonitions about what lay ahead for them.

Churchill was well prepared for his task having taken a continuous interest in service and defence matters during his time as a backbench MP. He had kept himself well briefed on developments by contact with serving officers and civil servants who, under the terms of the 1911 Official Secrets Act, took serious risks in reporting to him regularly on what they saw as the inadequacies of British rearmament. Much of this briefing covered air defence and radar rather than the navy and, at times, Churchill expressed simplistic views on sea power. He argued, for example, in January 1938 that 'the air menace,

left: Churchill in his map room.

left: the Graf Spee and right: the Graf Spee sinking.

against properly armed and protected ships of war will not be of a decisive character.'

From the first day of his return to the Admiralty he called for the fleet's role to be an offensive one, whatever the reservations of senior officers about its resources. Admiralty officers who voiced doubts about committing surface ships to action in the Baltic to disrupt German access to Scandinavian iron ore could find themselves quickly returned to seagoing duties. So too could those who queried some of their First Lord's high figures for claimed sinkings of U-boats over the winter of 1939-40. In a period of 'phoney war' the navy enjoyed a special prominence, either through disasters like the sinking of the Royal Oak in Scapa Flow in October 1939, or the spectacular chase of the German raider Graf Spee into the estuary of the River Plate where the captain scuttled his heavily damaged ship in December. Churchill made the most of the navy's successes, including the illegal boarding in Norwegian territorial waters of the Altmark in April 1940 to release British seamen held prisoner on it.

One threat to the navy's needs which Churchill had identified even before returning to office was the fact that the Irish state's 'treaty ports' on its northern and southern coasts would not be available to British ships. Under the 1921 treaty which created a self-governing Irish state, a Royal Navy presence in designated Irish ports was agreed to, but in 1938, after negotiations bitterly opposed by Churchill, these ports were given over to control by the de Valera government. This was a result of Chamberlain's correct assessment that Eire's neutrality in a war with Germany would be essentially benevolent to Britain. Churchill lost the argument over drawing up plans to re-take the ports, which would in the event have been of little strategic value after the fall of France in 1940 and the subsequent re-routeing of convoys to Britain around Ireland's northern coast.

This issue was one among many on which Churchill put his views to Chamberlain, often going well beyond his Admiralty brief. Despite his earlier antagonism to the Soviet state, he had become convinced by 1938 of the case for an alliance with Stalin to block Hitler's ambitions. Although he recognised that the August 1939 Moscow neutrality pact agreed to by the Soviet Union and Germany was a blow to Britain, by early September he presented a memorandum to Cabinet colleagues defending a Soviet presence in Eastern Poland under the pact's terms as a useful counterweight to Hitler's plans. He also began to talk of the Soviet Union's right to 'reclaim' territory lost after the First World War. When Finland was invaded by Stalin's forces on 30 November for refusing just such a demand, Churchill promptly changed his tune, calling for naval and military action to support the Finns and by extension, to disrupt Scandinavian iron ore shipments across the Baltic to Germany.

Chamberlain, whose commitment to a vigorous conduct of the war seemed to Churchill to be seriously lacking, bore his First Lord's numerous interventions and recommendations with weary patience. Churchill was still a heroic and impetuous figure who thought everyone should be like himself and nowhere was this clearer than in his continuing support for major naval operations in Scandinavian waters. The opportunity for this came closer when the Cabinet's Military Coordination Committee, of which Chamberlain had made him chairman, authorised in early April 1940 mine-laying operations off the coast of Norway.

This was quickly overtaken by Hitler's decision to invade Denmark and Norway, which in turn led to a large British naval force and a poorly-organised military expedition being sent to confront the Germans. With the element of surprise and good intelligence working for them, German troops rapidly took their main objectives. British, as well as French and Polish units, were ineffectively deployed against them and after serious losses were withdrawn from Norway well before the end of May, with only the port of Narvik being held for a little longer. Royal Navy losses were heavy and a grim reminder of the power of air attacks against surface ships but the German fleet suffered too, losing much of its surface strength. On the other hand, Hitler secured important bases for intensified air and U-boat attacks on Britain as well as access to crucial supplies of Swedish and Norwegian iron ore once Narvik was operating again. Churchill felt increasing frustration over events in Norway because, despite having the chair of the Military Coordination Committee, he sensed that the three armed services were neither being required to see the war as a whole nor getting the overall direction they needed from Downing Street.

The burden of criticism for what happened in Norway had to fall upon Chamberlain rather than Churchill, though he had supported action in Scandinavia since the start of the war. When on 7 May 1940 the House of Commons debated the campaign in Norway, Churchill loyally defended the government on the second day of the debate, despite a friendly warning from Lloyd George that he 'must not allow himself to be converted into an air-raid shelter to keep the splinters from hitting his colleagues.'

Churchill took his full share of the responsibility in a vigorous and eloquent speech in which he sought to talk up German losses and also the lessons learned by the navy. It was not enough to save Chamberlain who resigned once it was clear his normal majority in a motion to adjourn the house had fallen from 250 to 81.

Chamberlain made his decision on 9 May and early the next day Hitler launched his armies into Belgium and the Netherlands.

This gave added urgency to what recommendation as to his replacement he would make to King George VI. His preference was for his Foreign Secretary, Lord Halifax, but Churchill's clear unwillingness to serve under him, whatever he may previously have said, led the Labour leadership to withdraw its initial support for Halifax, subject to the support of their party's National Executive. Their backing came promptly but was arguably no more important than Halifax's disinclination to be Prime Minister.

Churchill did not carry out a coup in May 1940 nor was he swept into power by a great tide of public opinion though powerful elements of the press had been making the case for him. Writing soon afterwards, George Orwell argued that 'The people picked a leader nearer to their mood who was able to grasp that wars are not won without fighting.' Doubts about Churchill's maverick political record and his impetuous temperament were swept aside by the reality of German panzer divisions advancing relentlessly westward and by the new Prime Minister's serene sense of purpose. 'At last,' he recalled eight years later, 'I had the authority to give directions over the whole scene. I felt as if I were walking with destiny and that all my past life had been but a preparation for this hour and for this trial.'

Real fear about how Churchill might use this authority heightened the bitterness felt by those close to Chamberlain. 'We drank in champagne the health of the 'king over the water' (not King Leopold of Belgium, but Mr Chamberlain) wrote John Colville, a Downing street civil servant, in his diary entry for 10 May 1940. He went on to quote 'Rab', or

RA Butler, a junior minister at the Foreign Office, describing the new Prime Minister as a 'half-bred American supported by a rabble.' Seldom can a Prime Minister have taken office with so little support on the benches behind him in Parliament.

Yet the same diarist would write later of the impact Churchill achieved: 'within a fortnight all was changed. I doubt if there has ever been such a rapid transformation of opinion in Whitehall and of the tempo at which business was conducted. Government departments which under Neville Chamberlain had continued to work at much the same speed as in peacetime awoke to the realities of war. A sense of urgency was created in the course of a very few days and respectable civil servants were actually to be seen running along the corridors.' Changes

above: Neville Chamberlain.

like this were a signal of the huge energy which Churchill, already in his mid-sixties and still committed to a lifestyle of champagne, brandy, cigars and late hours which might have worn out many younger men, would bring to confronting the greatest crisis in Britain's history.

" LET US GO FORWARD TOGETHER"

CHAPTER 4

CHURCHILL AS PRIME MINISTER AND BRITAIN ALONE

JUNE 1940 – JUNE 1941

ALMOST TEN YEARS AFTER the war, in a speech to mark the occasion of his eightieth birthday, Churchill looked back to his years as Prime Minister and especially to the crisis of 1940. 'It was the nation and race dwelling all around the globe that had the lion's heart,' he told his audience. 'I had the luck to be called upon to give the roar.' This was one of many tributes he paid to the courage and endurance of the British people whom he had led but his 1940 speeches and broadcasts in response to events like Dunkirk, the Battle of Britain and the possibility of German invasion have never lost their power to move and stir those born long afterwards.

They are woven deeply into potent images of an offshore island of Europe confronting, alone and defiant, a triumphant Third Reich. Britain, of course, was not quite alone. Polish, Czech and Canadian crews flew against the Luftwaffe in August and September 1940, their aircraft had American-made precision instruments and engine parts, commonwealth states apart from Eire had rallied to Britain's cause and crucial economic aid in the form of

left: Poster 'Let us go forward together'.

above: RAF pilots awaiting an order to 'scramble' during the Battle of Britain.

left: WAAFs in an operations room. RAF flyers were dependent on the women in the Operations ('Ops') Rooms.

above: War Cabinet and the Ministers who regularly attended the full Cabinet;
Standing, left to right – Sir Archibald Sinclair, Mr Alexander, Lord Cranborne, Mr
Morrison, Lord Moyne, Captain Margesson, Mr Bracken,
Seated, left to right – Mr Bevin, Lord Beaverbrook, Mr Eden, Mr Attlee, Rt.Hon.Winston
Churchill, Sir John Anderson, Mr Greenwood, Sir Kingsley Wood.

Lend-Lease from the United States began to reach British shores early in 1941.

Even a lion's heart needed the hope of ultimate salvation which Churchill knew Britain on her own could not achieve and some of his greatest speeches in the 'invasion summer' were meant for an American as well as a British audience. In his 4 June 1940 Dunkirk speech, he told Parliament how, even if Britain was invaded and occupied, he would carry on the fight 'until, in God's good time, the New World, with all its power and might, steps forth to the rescue and liberation of the Old.'

His critics and detractors now argue that it was Japanese aggression at Pearl Harbour and not Churchill which brought the United States into the war and that the flow of economic aid from it to Britain which began in 1940 was simply part of a process by which a once-great economy lost its independence to the new power of America. Their special relationship may well have been one in which, by then, Britain was already living on borrowed time as a great power. Yet for Churchill and for Britain, survival and ultimate victory were the guiding priorities at this time and where desperately needed help came from was a lesser issue.

Revisionist historical writing has sought to strip away the layers of what is seen as the sacrosanct myth of 1940 which masks the realities of economic decline, dependence on America and acquiescence in the creation of a Soviet Empire in Europe once Stalin became an ally of Britain. Some contributors to this school of thought indeed argue that Churchill's historic error was to fight on in 1940 rather than seek terms with Hitler. There was in fact a peace party which

had a voice even within Churchill's War Cabinet. In May 1940 he had little choice but to retain as ministers appeasers like Chamberlain and Lord Halifax and to listen to their doubts about going on with the war.

On 15 May, the day before Churchill and his Cabinet authorised Operation Dynamo to evacuate the British Expeditionary Force from Dunkirk, Halifax talked to the Italian ambassador in London about possible mediation by Mussolini to halt hostilities with Germany. Three days later, with the evacuation under way, he made the case for Italian mediation as the basis for a cessation of hostilities. The four War Cabinet ministers were there, as well as Archibald Sinclair, the Liberal Party leader. There were hints and rumours of this at the time but only in 1970 did historians have legal access to the relevant Cabinet papers. Churchill

left: Churchill inspecting bomb damage at Coventry Cathedral.

had little choice but to permit a full debate, gambling on the fact that his Labour colleagues Clement Attlee and Arthur Greenwood would support him against Halifax, as would Sinclair. The key figure was Chamberlain, a sick and ailing man who would not live out the year. Initially he supported Halifax but flinched from splitting the Cabinet over his proposal.

This critical debate took place at a time when Churchill's position as Prime Minister was still insecure. When the Dunkirk evacuation began there was no certainty about its outcome and as a defeated army returned, rumours spread of an incompetently led campaign in France and Belgium. The writer JB Priestley, broadcasting on BBC radio on 5 June, invested Dunkirk with heroic and iconic status but Churchill knew it was a defeat and reminded ministers that 'wars are not won by evacuations.' What came to his rescue was the Battle of Britain and then the Luftwaffe's blitz on London and other cities.

These events enabled Churchill to isolate defeatism in high places by tapping into and giving voice to a powerful current of popular patriotism manifested by the million and a half men of all ages who, in the summer of 1940, joined the Local Defence Volunteers, or Home Guard, as they later became known. The Battle of Britain was immortalised by Churchill's tribute to RAF Fighter Command's pilots, the few to whom so many owed so much. Britain's fighter crews were not in fact outnumbered as heavily as legend would later claim, and had strategic advantages over the enemy, such as shorter operational distance to cover from their bases, as well as a radar

right: Viscount Halifax, British Secretary of State for Foreign Affairs.

early warning system. Factory production lines performed miracles to replace lost Spitfires and Hurricanes, but lost aircrew had to be replaced too and the margin of victory was always a narrow one as Churchill knew from his hour-by-hour contact with the battle.

The Battle of Britain, it has been said, moved seamlessly into the Blitz. On the night of 7 September, London began to burn as the Germans attacked it in strength for the first time. It went on burning for fifty seven consecutive nights as a ring of fire was drawn ever closer to the city's heart. Churchill remained at the epicentre of the battle in his Whitehall bunker though often placing himself in danger by viewing the action from the roof of the Treasury building above it. He knew

left: Churchill visits bombed Bristol. Behind him are Mrs Churchill and Mr Winant, the American Ambassador. He told the crowd 'We shall give it to them back.'

there were human limits to what people could endure and he grieved for their suffering. He was seen to weep at the sight of London's East Enders queuing to buy canary seed in what remained of their streets during a lull in the 1940 blitz and was visibly affected by the devastation and carnage in English ports like Plymouth as German raids intensified.

Churchill was aware, also, of populations abandoning bombed cities, often an immediate reaction to attack, especially in areas where shelter provision was inadequate and civilian emergency services overstretched. Negatives can be selected and stressed to support the view that Churchill led a people less heroic than he represented them to be in his speeches. Yet, as many accounts of the blitz show, after its initial horror, air attack taught people to adapt and endure and in many key industrial areas, output actually rose after major raids. Morale bent but never broke and Churchill was right to think of the people's courage as something more than just a creation of propaganda.

Few who worked with Churchill in these months of crisis were untouched by his dramatic injection of energy into the war's conduct. Meeting him, wrote RV Jones, the scientist who advised on the air war, gave 'the feeling of being recharged with a source of living power.' As important as these qualities, though arguably an extension of them, was Churchill's ability to develop a machinery of consultation and decision-making suited to the war's demands. His most important initial step was to take the title of Minister of Defence. There was no ministry as such but the move

left: Churchill inspecting a Tommy gun, 31 July 1940.
This image found its way into German hands and was later used as Nazi propaganda.

signalled his determination to exercise an overall control of decisions in a way that would minimise tensions between policy and strategy. A key figure was Major-General Sir Hastings 'Pug' Ismay, the Prime Minister's representative on the Chiefs of Staff Committee, who would brief him on its deliberations if and when he was unable to attend their meetings.

Senior to this body, however, was the Defence Committee (Operations) chaired by Churchill and usually attended by service ministers and Chiefs of Staff. The Foreign Secretary also sat on it and it was widely seen as the focal point for bringing together the political and military elements of grand strategy. Churchill also chaired the Defence Committee (Supplies) whose remit was to handle logistic issues, but which stayed in constant touch with the other committees. The Defence Committee (Operations) met less frequently as the war went on, but it remained as an outlet for doubts and dissent and a mechanism for restraint that could operate to control Churchill.

This could be necessary, given Churchill's restless and sometimes reckless preoccupation with new strategies and new weapons to shorten and win the war. These could be dangerously unrealistic, like his belief in an early 'Second Front' being opened in Norway and he had to be argued out of them. Even when that happened, he continued to respect the system he had brought into being as well as those prepared to disagree with him. No area of the war's conduct was immune from his scrutiny and his flow of minutes demanding 'action this day' became the stuff of legend.

He was prompt in creating ad hoc committees to focus in a dramatic way on specific aspects of the war. In June 1940, it was brought to his notice that the Germans had mastered the techniques of using radio beams to direct their aircraft to precise targets in Britain. RV Jones was at once summoned by Churchill to address a special meeting of ministers and service chiefs on the implications. The talented young scientist who had been seconded to the Air Ministry explained how it was possible to 'bend the beam' to divert attacks and Churchill acted at once. 'I gave all the necessary orders that very day,' he later wrote. 'The existence of the beam was to be assumed and all counter-measures were to receive absolute priority.'

The results were of huge importance in the air warfare over British cities which lay ahead and proof of Churchill's readiness to harness science and technology fully to the war effort. Similar proof came only a few months later when he set up a new emergency committee on U-boat warfare and the Battle of the Atlantic, the latter a stirring phrase he himself had coined. With Churchill the driving force from the committee's chair, service chiefs and scientists could bring under review every aspect of the grim struggle to keep the sea lanes open, settling inter-service disagreements and assessing expert evidence on how to neutralise the German submarine menace to Britain's survival.

Vital to both the war at sea and in the air was Britain's ability to interpret or decrypt Germany's Enigma machines through which encoded messages were sent by radio to German commanders in the field or at sea. This was how the

left: British troops return from action in Crete, after a disastrous attempt to hold the island against German airbourne landings.

Luftwaffe's use of the radio beam had been discovered in June 1940 and by early 1941 these 'Ultra' intercepts, made possible by the genius of specialist cryptographers at Bletchley Park, were picking up many more German secrets, including its plans to invade the Soviet Union, though Stalin did little with this information.

Intelligence gathering had always fascinated Churchill but he also appreciated the critical importance of this 'secret war' against Germany. Once in power he went some way to rationalise the various agencies involved. Out of this grew the Joint Intelligence Committee which coordinated and assessed secret intelligence. The vital 'Ultra' intercepts were, however, known only to a few people and were passed to Churchill several times a day in special yellow boxes to which he alone in 10 Downing Street had a key.

The abortive defence of Greece and Crete was undertaken in part by forces badly needed in North Africa. Churchill took the gamble, in late 1940, of committing sizeable British forces to offensive action against what he saw as a weak link on the Axis side. Major victories were won against poorly-led Italian forces both at sea and in the North African desert but at the price of formidable German forces being deployed in their support. Churchill hoped for quicker results than Sir Archibad Wavell, the Commander-in-Chief in the Middle East, could deliver. Wavell, who had endorsed intervention in Greece without necessarily foreseeing the logistic problems involved, never

achieved a close relationship with Churchill and was relieved of his command in June 1941.

By then, the blitz on Britain had passed its peak as Hitler concentrated air and ground forces for Operation Barbarossa, the invasion of the Soviet Union scheduled for late June 1941. Operation Sea Lion, the planned seaborne invasion of Britain had in fact been put on hold before the end of 1940. That, however, might not have happened without the will to resist shown by Britain's RAF and naval crews, the thousands who joined the new Home Guard and the civilian emergency services who helped London and other cities through the ordeal of the Blitz. Britain had survived the greatest crisis in its history and Churchill, in the panache and defiance of his leadership, came to personify that survival.

CHAPTER 5

THE TIDE TURNS

JUNE 1941 – JUNE 1944

Operation Barbarossa, Hitler's invasion of the Soviet Union on 21 June 1941, had been anticipated for some time by British intelligence services but its actual launch left Churchill little time to prepare his response. He worked for most of the following day on a broadcast which he only completed to his satisfaction twenty minutes before delivering it. 'No-one,' he reminded listeners, 'has been a more consistent opponent of Communism than I have been for the last twenty five years. I will unsay no word that I have spoken about it. But all this fades away before the spectacle which is now unfolding.' What followed was an eloquent evocation of a timeless peasant Russia once more confronting a brutal invader.

The struggle on the Eastern Front was indeed an awesome one, fought on a scale and with a ferocity which still drains the imagination. Hitler committed huge resources to

left: Churchill giving his trademark 'V for Vitory' sign.

destroy what he believed was a Jewish-controlled Bolshevist state. Against the Red Army he committed over 200 German divisions to battle and three-quarters of all German casualties were on the Russian front. During the siege of Leningrad, which was finally lifted in 1944, the city's death toll exceeded the combined British and American loss of life in the entire war.

It was the Soviet Union which broke the back of German military power but there were times when the struggle hung in the balance. Molotov, Stalin's Foreign Minister, knew this during his trip to London in May 1942, when he asked Churchill what Britain would do if the Red Army could no longer hold out. By then, the United States had joined the war and Churchill's reply was that, with its ever-increasing help, Britain would prevail. Without the Soviet Union, however, that would have taken much longer and would have cost infinitely more British and American lives. A German victory on the Eastern Front would moreover have brought back on to Hitler's agenda the unfinished business of invading Britain.

Churchill recognised the debt of blood which the wartime alliance with Stalin created, as indeed did his wife Clementine, who worked tirelessly in the cause of medical aid to the Soviet Union, but his relationship with the Soviet leader was never an easy one. Stalin never lost his suspicion of Churchill and in 1944 told the Yugoslav Communist Milovan Djilas that his 'ally' was the kind of man who will 'pick your pocket of a kopeck if you don't watch him.' The suspicion remained mutual but well before Barbarossa, Churchill knew the importance of the Soviet state joining the war and had set aside his own aversion to it. On the day following the German invasion, he assured a civil servant that 'if Hitler invaded Hell he would at least make a favourable reference to the Devil.'

The huge drama of the Russian front did not blind Churchill to the risks involved in the Soviet alliance, though his critics on the political right have now found historians who accuse him of refusing to see that the price of victory would be the emergence of a Soviet superpower with a predatory appetite. In reality Churchill, though sometimes wrong in his judgment of Stalin, tried hard, while putting ideological differences aside, not to accede mindlessly to his demands. These were soon apparent. In response to Britain's first offer, on 7 July 1941, of all possible aid, Stalin was soon pressing the case, not just for British landings in Europe but also for Churchill to send into the Soviet Union via Iran more divisions than were in combat readiness in the whole of the British Isles.

He also began to press for a British commitment to a joint approach with Stalin to any postwar settlement in Europe. Churchill had to tell him that this was impossible under the terms of the Atlantic Charter which he had agreed to with Roosevelt in August 1941 because it precluded either signatory power making bilateral agreements with other states. Churchill's first personal meeting with Stalin in Moscow in August 1942 was the most dramatic, though others followed. This was because he had to make clear to the Soviet leader that the Western allies were not ready for any Second Front in Europe to help the Red Army. He was subjected by his host to much denigration of Britain's war effort but answered him robustly. Angry exchanges alternated with somewhat ponderous bonhomie. At times, Stalin's brutal humour appalled Churchill, as when he joked with Roosevelt at the Teheran conference in November 1943 over whether the victorious allies should execute out of hand 50,000 or merely 49,000 captured German officers.

It was at Teheran that Churchill and Roosevelt finally gave Stalin the undertakings he wanted on European landings in 1944. By then, Churchill was playing a weakened hand because Roosevelt's military advisers wanted a decision and slow, costly progress by the allied armies in Italy was raising awkward questions about Churchill's preferred Mediterranean strategy. Churchill's problem lay in deciding what Stalin really wanted and how far to believe his protestations of loyalty to the Western alliance. These began to

wear thin in Churchill's mind as the crude reality of the man's demands for a Soviet-controlled postwar Polish state became apparent to him. Stalin showed himself happy to see the non-Communist Polish resistance crushed by the Germans in Warsaw in August 1944 and Poland did not figure in the 'percentages agreement' over postwar Western and Soviet spheres of influence agreed in October by the two leaders. Even so, with Hitler determined to fight on and with much of public opinion at home investing the Soviet Union and its leader with heroic status, Churchill, at least in public, had to act and talk as if he took Stalin at his word.

Early in the war before he became Prime Minister he spoke of Russia as 'a riddle wrapped in a mystery inside an enigma.' There was little need for him to think in such terms of Britain's other great wartime ally, the United States, or its

President, Franklin Roosevelt. Churchill had been disappointed in his hopes of Roosevelt throwing his country's weight behind the faltering attempts of Britain and France to halt Hitler's aggression prior to 1939. On taking office at the Admiralty when war came, one of his first acts was to write in warm personal terms to a man he had not met since 1918, when Roosevelt had been Secretary for the Navy. This marked the start of what became a huge correspondence between them once Churchill became Prime Minister.

Even as the German panzer divisions rolled westward in 1940, Churchill was clear in his own mind that while Britain might survive undefeated it would need allies like Russia and the United States to win the war. As events moved from crisis to crisis in the summer of that year, Churchill was quick to spell out for Roosevelt the implications of a British defeat and to appeal for all aid America could provide short of committing its own forces to battle. The urgency of such aid was heightened by the rate at which Britain's gold reserves were consumed in desperately needed arms purchases. Churchill, who considered himself to be half-American and with his affinity for things American, never doubted what the answer would be.

However, it had to be an answer kept on hold until Roosevelt had secured a third presidential term in the elections of November 1940. On 17 December, he announced that fifty American destroyers, many of them admittedly recently taken out of service because of age, would be made available to Britain. More dramatic by far was the President's broadcast of 29 December. In this, he called for his country to turn itself into the 'arsenal of democracy' and pledged his

above: British troops in action, in the North African desert, 1942.

support for a colossal programme to supply Britain with weapons, vehicles, machine tools and food under what became known as Lend-Lease. Between the enactment of the necessary legislation and the war's end, Britain received aid worth £5,000 million, a life support system for its war effort even if a down payment was demanded from what was left of its gold reserves.

Churchill did not let this blind him to the magnitude of what Roosevelt had done and on 12 March 1941, as Lend-Lease came on stream, he expressed his thanks at Westminster: 'In the name of his Majesty's Government and speaking, I am sure, for Parliament and for the whole country, and indeed in the name of all freedom-loving peoples, I offer to the United States our gratitude for her inspiring act of faith.' What Churchill wanted most

was America as a combatant and in January 1941, joint Staff Conversations opened in Washington, a crucial step in preparing for a joint war effort. Still however, he had to keep a tight rein on his hopes of America actually joining the war, especially after the high excitement of his August 1941 meeting with Roosevelt on the battleship *Prince of Wales* off Newfoundland.

Moving film footage survives of the two leaders singing together at a deck service, flanked by a ship's company of whom hundreds would die within a few months when their ship was sunk off Malaya by the Japanese. The Atlantic Charter signed at this meeting was not a treaty but a declaration of common purpose which contributed eloquently to the rhetoric of the fight against Hitler. Churchill knew that it was no substitute for an American

left: General Rommel's troops captured after a battle.

declaration of war. Despite increasing German U-boat attacks on American ships it was only the Japanese onslaught on Pearl Harbour which brought that about.

For two years after Pearl Harbour, certainly until the latter part of 1943, Churchill had good reason to think of his country's relationship with the United States as one of equality and common purpose. 'Tyranny is our foe', he told a Harvard University audience in September 1943, 'whatever trappings or disguise it wears, whatever language it speaks, be it external or internal, we must forever be on our guard, ever mobilised, ever vigilant, always ready to spring at its throat. In all this we march together.' Yet within the 'special relationship' disagreements had already surfaced.

Roosevelt listened to advisers who distrusted Churchill's belief that Britain must and could remain an imperial power, especially in India.

right: President Roosevelt meeting Churchill in Quebec. From left to right; Mr MacKenzie King (Prime Minister of Canada,) President Roosevelt and Churchill. On Roosevelt's death in April 1945, Churchill described him as 'the greatest American friend we have known.'

They also saw Churchill's imperial vision as an impediment to ending discriminatory trade practices and creating a multilateral postwar world economy. There were also divergent British and American priorities in the actual conduct of the war. These could involve intense and exhausting argument with Churchill initially gaining much of what he wanted. Agreement was achieved on a 'Europe first' strategy but Churchill saw merit in engaging German forces on the continent's periphery while Americans like Eisenhower and George Marshall, the US army Chief of Staff, believed large scale landings in France were essential.

Roosevelt backed Churchill over his case for American troops being used in Tunisia, Algeria and Morocco in late 1942, in support of British forces. The resulting thrust into Tunisia helped to end the war in North Africa but Churchill still needed American support for the invasion of Sicily. This was agreed at the Casablanca conference in January 1943 and it prepared the way for major landings in Italy. Churchill's Chiefs of Staff, especially Brooke, had their doubts, although they could see operations in Italy as a useful means of drawing German units into battle and securing airfields from which the Reich might be more deeply penetrated. By November, when the allies met at Teheran, Churchill was still holding out for a Mediterranean strategy despite the brutal loss-rate of the British and American armies in Italy. This conference however, was a turning point in the war because Stalin exploited disagreements between Churchill and Roosevelt to drive through the decision he wanted on an invasion of Europe.

Churchill had little option

but to accept, though with some flexibility conceded as to the precise date in May, 1944. Stalin made a promise, which he kept, of a massive Red Army offensive to back up the Allies when they landed. Teheran was a watershed in Churchill's relations with Roosevelt who had clearly gone there determined to talk directly to Stalin on his own terms and not Churchill's. He had also to agree reluctantly to Roosevelt's decision to land a major force in the South of France simultaneously with or close to the main invasion, with all the implications that had for the Italian front. Victory there could, in Churchill's view, take the Allied armies through the Ljubljana gap and into the Danube basin to avert postwar Soviet domination of Austria and Czechoslovakia. His view had some retrospective merit at the height of the Cold War but it is more

likely that such an effort would have weakened the Allies elsewhere, particularly when the priority for 1944 was Overlord, the code name for the landings in France.

Even with the Soviet Union and America as allies, disasters came thick and fast for Britain in the third year of the war. By the end of 1941, the Royal Navy's resources were stretched to breaking point in the fight to keep open Britain's sea lanes. Hitler may not have had a big enough fleet to cover an invasion in 1940 but his naval chiefs convinced him that Britain could be crippled by sustained air and U-boat attacks on the convoys that brought in the supplies upon which its survival depended. They came close to success, for at the start of 1942, Britain's imports were down to barely a third of their pre-war level. Only the dogged courage of her seamen and the brilliance of

overleaf: Churchill walks past a
Halifax Bomber.

cryptographers at Bletchley Park who in 1943 broke enough of the German codes to steer convoys clear of the stalking U-boat 'wolf packs', averted defeat on the Atlantic.

Churchill stayed in constant contact with this desperate battle, not just in Downing Street but by visiting ships and RAF Coastal Command squadrons as well as ports like Plymouth and Liverpool which played their part although devastated by sustained Luftwaffe attacks. In Plymouth in May 1941, he visited wounded men of the Royal Navy where they lay in a barracks, divided, as a civil servant later recalled, by only a low curtain from the coffins of the dead as they were being nailed down. In Cabinet he threw his weight behind every initiative and scientific development that could influence the struggle and in a secret session speech to Parliament on 25 June 1941, he paid tribute to 'the unconquerable, the inexhaustible adaptiveness and ingenuity of the British mind; the iron, unyielding, unwearying tenacity of the British character, by which we live, by which alone we can be saved, and by which we shall certainly be saved – and save the world.'

Pearl Harbour brought the world's second largest navy into the war on Britain's side but any immediate benefits from this were overshadowed by Japanese victories on sea and on land. In December 1941 Japanese aircraft operating off Malaya sunk the *Repulse* and the *Prince of Wales,* the latter being the ship which had carried Churchill to the Atlantic Charter meeting with Roosevelt. It was a savage reminder to him of the vulnerability of great surface ships to air attack, something he had taken time to be convinced of despite the destruction of the Italian fleet at Taranto in November 1940 by British carrier-based aircraft and of the Bismarck in May 1941, once it was crippled by air torpedoes.

Worse was to follow two months after Pearl Harbour, when Singapore fell to the Japanese on 15 February. Privately, Churchill blamed Australia for insisting on reinforcing its garrison beyond the point where the island could be defended. Yet he too had fallen into the trap of equating Singapore's role as a naval base with its potential as a fortress. Thousands of British and Dominion troops paid the price, either of death in battle or brutal captivity in Japanese hands, for the paucity of the island's defences. Churchill accepted his responsibility and later, in his history of the war, wrote of 'the hideous spectacle of an almost naked island' and declared 'I ought to have known. My advisers ought to have known and I ought to have been told. I ought to have asked.'

Japan's initially dramatic advances were halted by British and Indian forces in Burma and by the Americans and Australians in New Guinea. Huge air and naval battles on the south Pacific slowly turned the tide of war but Churchill's position for the first time since 1940 came under challenge when on 2 July 1942 he had to face a no-confidence motion in Parliament.

This failed, only twenty five members voting for it, but it was brought on by the loss of Tobruk to Rommel's Afrika Korps on 20 June. Britain's desert campaign had been faltering before that but Churchill intervened decisively, appointing General Bernard Montgomery to command the Eighth Army and visiting many of its units in Egypt before it launched its great counter-offensive at El Alamein in October.

For Britain until this point the war had been a matter of survival and Churchill was frustrated by the shortage of offensive options. One that he had high hopes of was strategic air power and in May 1942 the RAF had managed its first thousand-bomber raid of the war on Cologne. Churchill felt genuine horror at what the German blitz had done to London and other cities in 1940 but he has been accused of complicity in the way that this brutality was matched and surpassed once the RAF achieved the striking power to hit major urban targets. This was a product of the new Lancaster bomber's availability and of a ruthless and single-minded Bomber Command chief, Sir Arthur Harris, who had no problem in justifying the terrible firestorms his squadrons unleashed on cities such as Hamburg and Dresden.

Churchill's complicity in these attacks and in 'area bombing' more generally has been the subject of angry debate. The strategy cost the RAF appalling crew losses and it was a brutal business for the target cities. This Churchill never denied. Talking to Stalin in August 1942, two months after the Cologne raid, he said of the German population: 'We look upon its morale as a military target. We sought no mercy (he meant in 1940) and we would show no mercy.' So Bomber Command did not wage its war in some moral context unacceptable to Churchill and his ministers even if he began to distance himself from it and Harris in the war's final weeks. By then, like the Americans, its ability to hit precision targets was hugely improved but area raids had disrupted the German economy and tied up vital troops in anti-aircraft defence duty.

Where Churchill differed from Harris was in his scepticism about air power alone being able to win the war. That outcome, he always believed, would depend upon ground forces assaulting Hitler's 'fortress Europe.' His preference had been for using the Mediterranean theatre to do that, though he had also entertained perhaps exaggerated hopes of the ability of special forces to set 'Europe ablaze' by clandestine operations in support of resistance movements in occupied territories, or by frontal attacks like that on Dieppe in August 1942. This hideously ill-fated cross-Channel raid by British commando troops and Canadian units was in reality the prime responsibility of Lord Louis Mountbatten, a protegé of Churchill, promoted by him for his courage and panache from destroyer flotilla captain to the rank of Vice-Admiral in charge of Combined Operations.

Churchill generously took the full responsibility, later seeking to justify the operation as 'a costly but not unfruitful reconnaissance in force' from which useful lessons had been learned. Privately, Dieppe increased his premonitions about opening a second front in northern France. He often unburdened himself of his doubts to Eisenhower, the Supreme Commander of the Allies' invasion force, but by June 1944 he had overcome them and typically appalled King George VI by his declared intention to take part in the Normandy landings himself.

following page: Churchill inspects The First New Zealand Division.

right: Churchill and Roosevelt at the Casablanca conference, January 1943.

overleaf: Churchill cheered on arrival in the USA. Walking down a gangway of the vessel which brought him across the Atlantic, Churchill gives the 'V for Victory' sign in acknowledgement of cheers from Allied sailors and airmen as he arrives in the United States for conferences with President Roosevelt. Behind Churchill walks Vice Admiral Adolphus Andrews of the U.S. Navy.

following pages: On the way back from meeting Roosevelt, Churchill is greeted by Icelanders after visiting the Regent in Reykjavik. Walking behind Churchill is Ensign Franklin D. Roosevelt, Jnr., son of the American President.

right: Churchill and de Gaulle meet at Marrakesh, before reviewing French troops.

'This vain and malignant man.' was how Churchill once described de Gaulle. They admired each other, but their wartime relationship was sometimes a tense one because of the General's demand that his Free French government in exile be accorded parity with Britain's other allies.

CHAPTER 6

CHURCHILL ON THE HOME FRONT

'THIS IS NO WAR of chieftains, of dynasties or national ambition; it is a war of peoples and causes. There are vast numbers not only in this island but in every land, who will render faithful service in this war, but whose names will never be recorded. This is a war of the Unknown Warriors.' With these words in a broadcast he gave on 14 July, 1940, Churchill seemed to many of his listeners to be invoking the concept of a 'People's War' against Hitler. Some historians have argued that this was indeed what the war quickly became. Whether Churchill thought through the full implications of what he was saying is another matter.

Other popular wartime communicators like the novelist JB Priestley did exactly this in his contribution to the BBC's Sunday evening talks series called Postscript. He made his debut on 5 July, just as

left: Churchill watching anti-aircraft guns in action.

the Dunkirk evacuation was completed and developed an increasingly populist style. He talked about the war and its sacrifices being justified not just by victory over Hitler but by the goals of real social justice and the assertion of the values of community over those of property. Churchill shared the alarm which began to be voiced by some influential Conservatives but Priestley survived, continued his talks into October 1940 and indeed contributed a further series the next year.

These talks were hugely popular and in the view of the novelist Graham Greene, Priestley 'became in the months after Dunkirk a leader second only in importance to Mr Churchill.' They were symptomatic of a wartime mood which was shifting slowly but perceptibly amidst the fears and hardships of the invasion summer and the Blitz. It would take time before this sea-change would be a threat to Churchill. Through 1941 and 1942 he maintained a unique and, given his background and history, an improbable rapport with the British people, never condescending to them in his speeches and broadcasts yet dramatising for them their role, however small, in an epic and honourable struggle.

Churchill loved cinema and was happy for the Ministry to throw its support behind talented film directors whose work would celebrate Britain's war effort and the democratic patriotism which under-pinned it. Among the results were 'In Which We Serve' directed by David Lean as a tribute to the Royal Navy; 'The Way Ahead', a rousing but also thoughtful film on Britain's citizen army directed by Carol Reed and Frank Launder's and Sidney Gilliat's

'Millions Like Us' focussing on women aircraft production workers.

Another of the Ministry's functions was to monitor civilian morale through its Home Intelligence Units, though it also increasingly used non-governmental agencies such as Mass Observation, set up by Tom Harrisson before the war to study and record British lifestyles and social mores. This work of course extended to what was thought to be the impact on public opinion of media coverage of the war as well as of feature films.

Churchill however was by temperament capable of jumping in ahead of these agencies. In March 1942, he was enraged by a cartoon in the Daily Mirror, already enjoying huge sales. Drawn by Philip Zec, this powerfully depicted a torpedoed sailor clinging to a raft in a menacing and empty sea.

The caption, written by the paper's renowned columnist William Connor, read: 'The price of petrol has been raised by a penny (Official).'

This could be read as implying that Royal and Merchant Navy crews were risking their lives to bring in desperately-needed fuel supplies only for profiteers to force up the price. The Mirror's chairman and editor were severely censured by Churchill's government and warned that their paper could be suppressed. Churchill had the power to do this and had already used it to close down the British Communist Party's Daily Worker in 1941. Using it against the Mirror, with its massive sales, would have been folly. Unions speaking for journalists and print workers mobilised in protest and Churchill accepted the need for retreat.

The Zec cartoon had coincided with a critical stage of the Battle of the Atlantic but he was not the only cartoonist whose work provoked a reaction from Churchill. Another was the New Zealand-born David Low, who in 1934 had launched, in the London Evening Standard, Colonel Blimp, a rotund figure with drooping white moustache who symbolised upper class military incompetence. The word Blimp became a standard one in newspaper coverage of the war which was at all critical and in 1942 the film director Michael Powell decided, at a time when British armies were in retreat on every front, to bring the Colonel to cinematic life in a film called 'The Life and Death of Colonel Blimp.'

Powell's purpose was to tell the story of a fictional officer who first saw action in the Boer War and then rose by 1939 to the rank of general. The film, now rated a classic, made affectionate fun of its hero but its message was a serious one, that a war against German Fascism could not be won by the gentlemanly assumptions and outdated rules of Colonel Blimp. When Churchill learned of the film being in production, he minuted angrily to Bracken, the Information Minister, in September 1942: 'Pray propose to me the measures necessary to stop this foolish production before it gets any further. I am not prepared to allow propaganda detrimental to the morale of the army and I am sure the Cabinet will take all necessary action.'

Bracken patiently talked Churchill out of an ill-judged act of censorship and the film script was vetted and passed by the Ministry. Episodes like these show both Churchill's weaknesses and his strengths. On the home front, as in the wider conduct of the war, he was all too capable of over-reaction but he could also listen to good advice and accept it without rancour. The Colonel Blimp case is a reminder too that he grasped the huge importance of the wartime media without having fully worked out what their role should be.

This role became ever more important as the political landscape began to change. Full employment and a managed economy created by the war, along with the rhetoric and reality of sacrifice in a common cause made it hard for Churchill to ignore a growing debate on postwar social policy. In fact, he made some effort to stay in control of this debate without getting too much drawn into the detail. Cabinet papers began to flow on every aspect of the debate and in 1941 Churchill set up an inter-departmental committee to examine social insurance and allied services.

Its chairman, Sir William Beveridge, a prickly and egocentric civil servant, had wanted a major job in Ernest Bevin's Ministry of Labour. Bevin was not alone in disliking Beveridge and thought that the chairmanship of the new committee would serve to marginalise his influence. This proved to be one of the great political miscalculations of the war, for within two years the Beveridge Committee produced a report which set out the essential building blocks of Britain's postwar Welfare State.

overleaf: Churchill with Clement Attlee and Anthony Eden, walking along a London station platform, 19 August 1941.

'A modest man with much to be modest about.' This unjustly dismissive remark, is said to have made by Churchill about Attlee. In reality, he valued Attlee and Labour's support in the coalition government and trusted him as his deputy.

People queued in foul weather to buy copies of the report and its sales were spectacular. Beveridge became a somewhat incongruous public hero in ceaseless demand by the press and radio. This reaction caught Churchill badly off balance. His earlier credentials as a social reformer, by which he laid much store, precluded any rejection of a report which appeared to lay out a strategy for slaying the 'five giants' of want, disease, ignorance, squalor and idleness, the last being Beveridge's preferred word for unemployment.

The report called for the financing of social services by contributory funding rather than by Labour's formula of redistributive taxation. It made no claims that the trade cycle could be controlled to eliminate unemployment for good and its view of women's role in the labour market was a patriarchal one.

Even so, in calling for such measures as a health service free to all at the point of need, as well as family allowances, Beveridge seemed to convert wartime rhetoric into attainable goals.

In his history of the war, Churchill made little reference to the Beveridge Report but he did quote a memorandum he wrote to his ministers in January 1943, warning them of a dangerous optimism which he felt could build up over the type and scope of social legislation that could be afforded in postwar conditions. He held to this position as the groundswell of support for Beveridge developed. His doubts went beyond finance, for the report took a 'universalist' view of providing a minimum standard of support for all classes, while his conception of welfare had always been a more selective one, rooted in a 'safety net' role for the state in protecting society's casualties.

Churchill's response to Beveridge was, arguably, consistent with his own record on social legislation, but in public he followed the Treasury's line on the rashness of over-ambitious postwar commitments. So too did the new Cabinet Committee on Reconstruction Priorities which he set up in January 1943. By this time, though, the Coalition Conservative vote was starting to come under challenge in a series of contested by-elections in which the Beveridge plan loomed large as an issue. The Coalition government parties abided by an agreement that they would not fight each other for Parliamentary seats which became vacant, but this did not stop independents or Common Wealth, a new radical grouping formed in 1941, from entering the fray.

In Parliament too, cynicism about the coalition's intentions on Beveridge was expressed in hostile votes when the plan was debated in February 1943. A total of 119 members, nearly all Labour, went into the 'No' lobby on the issue of implementation. This was a revolt which dwarfed the Tobruk vote seven months previously and Churchill began to adopt a more conciliatory tone. In a broadcast the following month, he held to his case against a binding commitment to Beveridge but did speak of a 'Four Year Plan' for social legislation after Hitler's defeat. This plan, he stressed, would provide for extended social insurance, educational reform and health care.

This caution by Churchill had political implications which his huge responsibilities for the overall conduct of the war made it difficult

for him to grasp. The Beveridge debate had sharpened many people's expectations of the changes victory could bring. A May 1944 White Paper on employment policy went some way to match this mood, although the instruments it proposed for maintaining a high level of postwar employment were weaker than John Maynard Keynes, the great economist and adviser to the government, would have wished.

Even for Churchill, by the latter part of the war it was becoming difficult to hold his party in line behind an increasingly interventionist legislative agenda. There was open dissent over strategies pressed for by Labour in the coalition to control profits from the postwar development of urban and rural land, while with Ernest Bevin's bill to set minimum standards of protection for notoriously underpaid catering workers, Conservative members in Parliament tried to block its enactment. The contours of postwar party battles were beginning to be drawn. Churchill was slow to see it but so too was the Labour leadership. Bevin, though, later recalled that as he watched British troops sail for Normandy in June 1944, one soldier spotted him and shouted: 'See they don't let us down this time.' It was a message which Churchill also needed to hear.

left: Women production workers, producing Spitfire parts. In September 1943, Churchill told a London audience 'war has taught us to make vast strides forward towards a far more complete equalisation of the parts to be played by men and women in society.

overleaf: Churchill and his daughter Mary watching anti-aircraft guns being fired.

CHAPTER 7

VICTORY IN THE WEST AND POLITICAL DEFEAT AT HOME

1944-1945

'YOU WILL ENTER the Continent of Europe and undertake operations aimed at the heart of Germany and the destruction of her armed forces. You are about to embark upon the Great Crusade towards which we have striven these many months. The hopes and prayers of liberty-loving people everywhere are with you.' This was General Dwight Eisenhower's communiqué to the men of the Allied invasion force under his supreme command who finally set off by sea and by air late on the evening of 5 June 1944, or in the early hours of the next morning, for the invasion of Normandy.

Churchill was not among them, having given way to his sovereign's strongly expressed wish that he should not put himself at risk. Typically, he went ashore six days after D-Day to visit the British and Canadian front and to talk to

left: The Big Three Conference: Churchill meets Truman. 'I am sure we can get along fine if he doesn't try to give me too much soft soap.' This was Truman's laconic view of Churchill after he succeeded Roosevelt to the Presidency in April 1945. Their working relationship was cut short by Churchill's election defeat in July.

above: Montgomery. Church bells rang throughout the land to mark General Bernard Montgomery's victory over the German Afrika Korps at El Alamein in late October 1942. He went on to command British and Canadian forces in the invasion of Europe in 1944 and retained Churchill's trust though his American allies often found him difficult to work with.

Montgomery who commanded it. He also took special satisfaction in witnessing the shelling of German positions by the Royal Navy destroyer which had taken him across to the invasion beaches. The Allies, especially the Americans, had already sustained serious losses but a bridge-head had been secured. Superior air and naval firepower were crucial as were the two Mulberry harbours, vast prefabricated structures of steel and concrete, towed across the Channel to provide secure landing facilities for reinforcements and supplies until such time as serviceable parts were in Allied hands.

Even so, the fighting in Normandy was bitter and costly. Hitler, unlike Von Rundstedt, his commander in the West, had guessed correctly where the Allies would land but failed to act upon his intuition, holding back the powerful 15th Army

north of the River Seine, while the Allies tightened their grip on ground secured since D-Day. When the 15th Army, with its formidable Panzer units, was committed to battle late in July, it was too late. German forces had been ground down by Allied firepower though they still used the winding lanes and high hedgerows of Normandy's bocage country to brutal defensive effect. Breakout for the Allies came in early August when they finally encircled and destroyed a critical number of German divisions in the Caen-Falaise pocket.

News of victorious armies rolling westwards from Normandy across France and into Belgium and Holland raised the spirits of British people. Radio, press and cinema gave them reports of euphoric scenes from liberated cities. Unconditional surrender, demanded of Germany since the January 1943 conference at

Right: Churchill,
Roosevelt and Stalin at
the Yalta Conference,
February 1945.

Casablanca began to seem attainable and might have been achieved if airborne forces dropped in Holland in September could have taken all the bridges on the river system which intersected the country. It was not to be and attritional battles had to be fought both by the western allies and the Red Army before the German Reich itself could be penetrated.

A further ordeal also confronted people in London and southern England: just seven days after D-Day the first German flying bomb landed. It was the first of the V1s, Hitler's secret weapon. Two thousand followed in the next fortnight, resulting in heavy loss of life and in early September the V2s began to hit the capital city. The V1 was a pilotless plane carrying a bomb but the V2 was a sophisticated rocket flying too high for RAF fighters to intercept it. A million people were evacuated from London and Churchill showed signs of real strain as the death toll mounted.

In reality, Hitler's claims for the potential of these weapons were excessive, though they were a triumph of German science and technology and heralded a new military era of guided missile systems. They were developed and deployed at a point in the war when the Wehrmacht on the ground was dangerously short of more basic weapons and of adequate fuel for its vehicles. As Professor Richard Overy wrote in his book *Why the Allies Won*, Hitler's scientists pursued excellence for its own sake and tried to win the war with the weapons of the 1950s when what was really needed was effective output of the weapons of the 1930s.

This, of course, is a perspective from which historians can now view

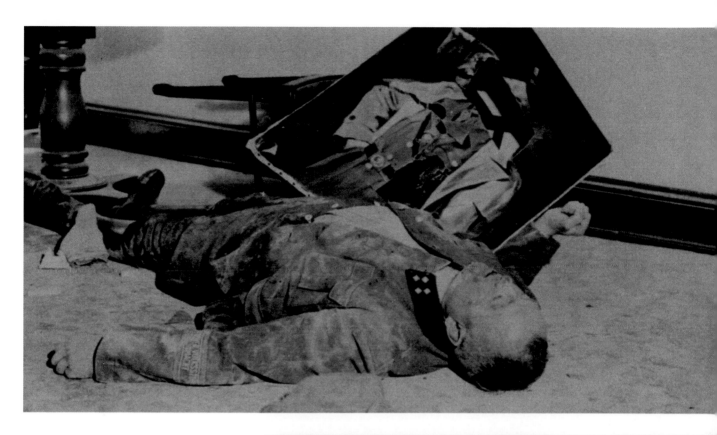

above: As Allied troops advance to Berlin, this local party leader has committed suicide, having first defaced a painting of Hitler.

right: Field Marshal Wilhelm Keitel signs the ratified surrender terms at Soviet headquarters in Berlin, 9 May 1945.

left: Churchill at Armistice Day Parade in Paris, 11, November 1944. Churchill and de Gaulle lay wreaths on the tomb of France's unknown soldier at the Arc de Triumphs in Paris, on Armistice Day. Afterwards they walked down the Champs Elysees and were given a tremendous reception from the huge crowd. Mr Eden is immediately behind Churchill.

Anthony Eden was a loyal colleague to Churchill as his Foreign Secretary during the Second World War and again from 1951 to 1955, but he became frustrated by his long wait to succeed Churchill as Prime Minister, which he finally did when his leader retired in April 1955.

the matter. For Churchill, feeling the physical and mental strain of leadership as the war entered its sixth year, the V1 and V2 attacks represented a crisis. There was desperate talk by him of intensifying the destruction of German cities by the RAF and of recourse to poison gas or even anthrax. Experimentation with the latter indeed predated the flying bomb and rocket attacks whose indiscriminate nature appalled and enraged Churchill. In a memorandum to ministers in July 1944, he set up a case for at least considering extreme counter measures against a barbaric enemy: 'I do not see why we should have all the disadvantages of being gentlemen while they have all the advantages of being the cad.' The crisis eased as the bombs and missile sites were overrun by British troops and on 1 March 1945 Churchill issued the necessary order to halt work on both poison gas bombs and on anthrax.

By then plans to cross the Rhine were being made by the British and American armies and victory was in sight. Churchill's preoccupations were already shifting increasingly to the form and content of a postwar settlement acceptable to the Western allies and the Soviet Union. In early February he had travelled to Yalta in the Crimea to meet Stalin and Roosevelt. Churchill no longer had a strong hand to play because a terminally ill Roosevelt was desperate to ensure that Stalin would soon join the war against Japan. The price he was ready to pay for this was meaningless promises about elections and multi-party democracy in Poland and other countries where the war's final campaigns clearly guaranteed a Soviet military presence.

Agreements were however,

reached with Stalin over co-ordinating the final offensives against Germany and over its occupation by the victors. Churchill returned from the toasts and banquets at Yalta to defend these agreements in Parliament as well as a three-power declaration on postwar co-operation by the signatories and the rights of liberated states. He still wanted to believe Stalin's word and there was little opposition to his statement from MPs.

Yalta was Churchill's last meeting with Roosevelt, who died on 12 April. Five days later he paid a heartfelt tribute to him in Parliament, describing him as 'the greatest American friend we have ever known and the greatest champion of freedom who has ever brought help and comfort from the New World to the Old.' The two leaders' relationship had been a remarkable one, yet much of what was hoped for from it – such as the shared development of atomic power and the creation of a multilateral economy – did not come to pass. Nonetheless, Hitler's defeat could not have been achieved without the United States. Churchill had always known this, though it was hard for him to accept how the 'special relationship' had altered. At the outset of their wartime partnership, the two allies were closer to each other in military power than would ever be possible in a post-war world in which, despite the onset of the Cold War, the complexity of their interests would make each a less essential partner of the other.

Churchill worked quickly to build a good relationship with Roosevelt's successor Harry Truman

overleaf: Churchill being cheered in liberated Antwerp.

and was able to savour with him the final victory secured amidst the rubble of Berlin and by the converging advances across the Reich of the Allied armies. The news of the German surrender reached Churchill early on the morning of 7 May. Always mindful of his compatriots' essential needs, he made sure that London's pubs would not run short of beer and authorised a Board of Trade announcement that the public could buy red, white and blue bunting without coupons until the end of the month. In early afternoon, Churchill was driven to Buckingham Palace, outside which an enormous multitude had gathered. From the palace balcony, standing with the King, the Queen and their daughters, he spoke as Big Ben struck three. He confined himself to a brief announcement of the surrender terms and their signatories but then, to a huge roar

from his audience, he added: 'The evildoers now lie prostrate before us. Advance Britannia!'

For Churchill, past his seventieth birthday and the survivor of heart trouble and a serious attack of pneumonia in 1943, victory brought little remission from the demands of leadership. The war with Japan was still to be won and even before the German surrender he was beginning to voice his anxieties about Soviet intentions. Writing on 4 May to Anthony Eden, the Foreign Secretary, he declared that 'Russian demands in Germany for reparations alone will be such as to enable her to prolong the occupation almost indefinitely, or at any rate for many years, during which time Poland will sink with many other states into the vast zone of Russian-controlled Europe.' Three days later, in a telegram to Truman, Churchill made his first use of the 'iron curtain' metaphor to describe the divisions beginning to harden between the Western powers and Soviet-controlled Europe.

Despite this, his final meeting with Stalin at Potsdam in Berlin in July was accompanied by much camaraderie, though only a few Soviet concessions were secured over troop withdrawals from Iran and a Western role in the occupation of Vienna. Churchill's relationship with Stalin had grown out of brutal imperatives for both of them and was never a real basis for the long term trust which at times he had thought might develop from it.

It was also at Potsdam that Churchill gave his consent to the use of the atomic bomb against Japan. Although he had agreed three years earlier to the pioneering atomic research of British scientists being shared with the Americans, the final decision was Truman's. 'I never doubted that it would be,' he later wrote, 'nor have I ever since doubted that he was right.' Japan was working intensively on its own atomic weapons programme as well as ruthlessly pursuing germ warfare research using prisoners for experimentation. Even with its oil supply virtually gone, there is little doubt that Japanese forces would have fought on with whatever means they had if their islands had been invaded by the Allies.

The bombs dropped on Hiroshima and Nagasaki after Churchill had left office brought an abrupt end to the war in the Far East, while also demonstrating to the world that a grim new age of overkill had arrived. Group Captain Leonard

overleaf: the Big Three Conference: Churchill tours Berlin, July 1945.

Cheshire V.G., the much-decorated RAF bomber pilot, flew over Nagasaki as an observer when the second bomb was dropped and was haunted by the memory of what he had seen. 'We realised,' he later wrote, 'that a new age had begun and possibly we had all made some contribution to raising a monster that could consume us all.' Churchill came to understand that too as some of his final speeches in Parliament ten years later would show.

On the evening of 25 July 1945, Churchill retired for the night almost as serenely as he had done after taking office five years earlier. The outcome of Britain's first General Election in ten years would be known the next day. Voting at home had been on 5 July, but a final result had to allow time for the votes of some three million members of the British forces, many of them serving over-

seas, to be counted. Conservative General Office had advised the Prime Minister to expect a substantial majority and he accepted the party manager's complacency. It seemed but a short step to reconstituting the coalition and carrying on in office with the mandate of a grateful people.

Later, in the final volume of his war history, Churchill recalled how his confidence had begun to ebb away during the night. 'Just before dawn,' he wrote,' I woke suddenly with a sharp stab of almost physical pain. A hitherto subconscious conviction that we were beaten broke forth and dominated my mind.' He slept fitfully for another hour or two before taking breakfast and arrived in his underground maproom at 9.00am, where the first results were coming in. By noon, he was clear in his own mind that a Labour majority was in the making. Over a sulphurous lunch,

Clementine tried to humour him by suggesting that the result might be a blessing in disguise. 'At the moment it seems quite effectively disguised' was Churchill's growled, but now famous retort.

The magnitude of Labour's victory surprised its leadership. Clement Attlee who had been Deputy Prime Minister in the Coalition, was a famously taciturn man who typically gave away little in his memoirs about what he had really expected. He did admit that he had the better of the exchanges between himself and Churchill during the campaign and was gratified, as a cricket-lover, by one account of the election which described his duel with Churchill as that of 'a sound and steady batsman keeping up his wicket against a demon bowler who was losing both pace and length.'

What helped to deceive Churchill about the likely result was the popular acclaim which greeted him in so many places and he put much of the emphasis of his speeches and broadcasts on how voters could safely entrust major postwar social legislation to him and his party. In coalition, he pointed out, they had already delivered Family Allowance and an ambitious Education Act and he offered them his vision of an enterprise-based economy and a benignly interventionist state guiding Britain into a new era of peace. His crucial mistake was to allow this message to be drowned by his increasingly virulent attacks on Labour and its leaders, the very men who, like Attlee, had been valued colleagues in government only a few weeks earlier. For many voters this was Churchill reverting to type and his 4 June broadcast in which he predicted a Labour Gestapo in

left: Part of the huge area of Nagasaki, swept clear of buildings by the blast of an atom bomb, the second to be dropped by the Americans on Japan in 1945.

Churchill supported Truman's decision to use atomic weapons against Japan, but came to fear their use in any war between the West and the Soviet bloc.

Britain, confirmed their fears. It was made against the advice of his wife and would not have been made at all if his daughter Sarah, serving with the WAAF, had written sooner the letter she sent him the day after the broadcast. In it she told him of the ordinary people she had met during the war and of their modest hopes for a better world. 'Socialism as practised in the war did no-one any harm and quite a lot of people good,' she stated, pleading, 'cannot this common sharing and feeling of sacrifice be made to work as effectively in peace?' Her fellow servicemen and women, she warned him, while rejecting totalitarianism, would still vote Labour in sizeable numbers, as indeed they did.

The decisive swing away from the Conservatives had in fact started long before this and can be measured from wartime by-elections and early exercises in opinion polling. Labour, without its leaders fully realising it, was in a position to place itself at the head of a rising tide of generous progressive thinking which it had helped to shape and to which the common hopes and sacrifices of the war had given a powerful moral ascendancy. It is easy to argue now that Churchill should have read the danger signals sooner, but his role as a national leader in a global conflict had made relentless demands upon him. If he failed to read them it was in part because he had delegated much of the responsibility for Home Front policy to colleagues, often Labour ones, while he grappled with awesome decisions and struggled to maintain an equal relationship between Britain and two emerging superpowers.

When the election count was

complete, Labour had won 393 seats in the House of Commons and had a majority of 146 over all other parties. Its share of the total vote cast was 48 per cent. Traditional areas of heavy industry loyal to Labour had joined forces with the newer areas of South East England and the West Midlands. George Orwell, in his essay *The Lion and the Unicorn* identified the junior managers and skilled workers recruited by light industry in such places as an indeterminate social group, not instantly placeable by clothes or accents, who had been politicised by the war and were ready to trust Labour.

The result was a bitter blow to Churchill, but he never resorted to the kind of language of Conservatives such as the socialite and diarist Sir Henry Channon. On 28 July he wrote of how he was 'shocked and stunned by the country's treachery.' For a somewhat late convert to Churchill's cause in 1940 this was perhaps an extravagant reaction. Churchill himself showed more magnanimity to the electorate than he had done to some of his former Labour colleagues during the election campaign. After conceding defeat, he said 'It only remains for me to express to the British people, for whom I have acted in these perilous years, my profound gratitude for the unflinching, unswerving support which they have given me during my task, and for the many expressions of kindness which they have shown towards their servant.'

following pages: **VE-Day;** Waving to the crowds from Buckingham Palace. Left to right: Princess Elizabeth (Queen Elizabeth II), Queen Elizabeth (the Queen Mother), Churchill, King George VI, Princess Margaret. following page: View from behind Churchill waving to the crowds.

CHAPTER 8

OPPOSITION, RETURN TO POWER AND THE SOVIET THREAT

1945–1965

Loss of power did not tempt Churchill even to consider retirement, regardless of his wife's wishes. This produced some strain in their relationship as did the difficulties of their now grown-up children. Mary, the youngest, entered into a happy marriage in 1947, but her brother Randolph and two older sisters caused their parents much distress with both alcoholism and divorce. One of them, Sarah, committed suicide in 1963.

Amidst these family storms, travel and painting provided badly-needed relaxation. Laying down the burdens of leadership also gave Churchill time to start writing again and between 1948 and 1954 he completed his hugely successful six-volume history of the war. Its sales made him a relatively wealthy man and it has never been out of print. The complete series was published in fifty countries and serialised world-wide in eighty newspapers and

left: Churchill, in RAF uniform, 1948.

magazines. Between 1956 and 1958 he also finished his *History of the English Speaking Peoples*, by which time he had been honoured with the Nobel Prize for Literature.

His lack of relish for the often mundane rituals of opposition in Parliament was apparent after 1945 but there was still a role for him on the world stage, especially because of the Cold War and his readiness to act as the custodian of Britain's alliance with America. His oratory had lost none of its resonance and at Fulton, Missouri, on 5 March 1946, he delivered one of the great speeches of the early postwar period. It tends now not to be interpreted by historians as a turning point in the Cold War but rather as an event highlighting the Truman administration's ambivalence about relations with the Soviet Union.

The speech is remembered above all for one dramatic sentence: 'From Stettin in the Baltic to Trieste in the Adriatic an iron curtain has descended across the Continent.' Churchill had no copyright on this phrase but he used it with great effect, arguing that from behind this curtain the Soviet Union sought 'the fruits of war and the indefinite expansion of their power and doctrines.' He was also emphatic on the point that this was not tantamount to a desire for war with the West. Peace, he stressed to his Fulton audience, could be maintained by a strong United Nations, supported to the full by Britain and the United States.

The American media in the main were sceptical or hostile and Truman had to disclaim prior knowledge of the speech. In London the Times ran an editorial critical of Churchill but leading members of the Labour Cabinet agreed with its

left: Churchill on holiday at port of St Jean De Luz, South of France, 16 July 1945.

above: Marshal Pétain, a war hero and military ally of Churchill from the
First World War, on trial for running the Vichy government, 1945.

Churchill had recognised Pétain's role as a saviour of France in 1916, but when he met
him in the French cabinet in the crisis of June 1940, he recalled the aged Marshal being
'mockingly incredulous' at his appeals to France to fight on. Soon after this, Pétain took
power and embarked upon a collaborationist peace with Hitler which in 1945 brought
him to trial charged with treason against his country. He was sentenced to life
imprisonment and died in 1951.

above: Pierre Laval, giving evidence at Pétain's trial. Laval had been Prime Minister of Vichy France. He was executed, after having been found guilty.

general thrust, especially Bevin, the Foreign Secretary. He took a much more imperial view of Britain's post-war role than Attlee and felt that American support was essential if British power in the world was to be maintained. This certainly influenced Churchill's thinking. Recent work on post-1945 British foreign policy points to his concern with the American alliance being driven as much by fear for the future of an empire which could only be held together with American acquiescence, if not support, as by fear of the Soviet Union.

Growing domestic anti-Communism and spy hysteria would have altered the direction of American policy without Churchill's Fulton speech. Yet, despite its luke-warm reception in the United States at the time, the speech may yet have helped to prepare American opinion for the interventionist role in Europe soon to be embodied by the Marshall Plan and support for the North Atlantic Treaty Organisation.

Churchill welcomed these bold American initiatives, but did not seem to see that a revitalised and democratic Western Europe was viewed by Washington as having the potential to become as important a partner as Britain alone. The Marshall Plan and the start of a movement towards closer economic and political relationships among European states

---

right: The Nuremberg trial of the Nazi leadership, began in October 1945 and ended a year later: left to right Göring, Hess and von Ribbentrop. Göring was sentenced to death, but committed suicide just before his execution. Hess was sentenced to life imprisonment and von Ribbentrop was hanged.

Churchill had not initially been in favour of trials but was persuaded by the Americans that such a process was important.

left: front of Chartwell, Churchill's home from 1922. Overlooking the Weald of Kent, it became the family home for the next 40 years. During the war, the house was shut down as it was in the direct flight path of Nazi bombers and Churchill lived in Downing Street and Chequers. He would come down for a night or two, but would not sleep in the main building. After Churchill's death in 1965, Clementine did not wish to continue living in the house, so the house and many pieces of furniture, carpets and *objects d'art* were also bequeathed to the nation.

overleaf: Chartwell.

were developments Churchill could applaud, but, no more than the Attlee government did he seem able to see a role for Britain in the emergence of a new grouping of states in the West.

As early as September 1945, Churchill had commended to a Zurich audience the need for 'a kind of united states of Europe', citing the success of Switzerland over the years in federating its cultural and linguistically diverse cantons. General Charles de Gaulle, then Prime Minister of France after the years of his often tense wartime relationship with Churchill reacted by arguing that any form of European union needed France and Britain as founder members, though Churchill's speech had made no reference to this.

Ironically, de Gaulle would later use his veto power as President of France to keep Britain out of the European Common Market created by the 1957 Rome Treaty. Churchill had retired by then and his rhetorical enthusiasm for Europe – expressed in postwar speeches to the new Council of Europe – never converted itself into any substantial policy initiatives, either as his party's leader in opposition or as Prime Minister again after 1951. This became a cause of frustration to many of his closest colleagues who failed to see that in reality his conception of Europe was similar to that of de Gaulle. Both of them believed passionately in the integrity of the nation state.

Western European military co-operation against the Soviet threat was, however, something Churchill did support even if it meant the rearmament of West Germany. For this he earned the gratitude of Konrad Adenauer, the wily old Rhenish patriarch who became its Chancellor in 1949. Achieving it was a tortuous

above: Churchill became something of a builder and took to
bricklaying, building walls around his estate at Chartwell.
This plaque commemorates his achievements.

above: Chair at Chartwell donated by well wishers.

process. When back in office after 1951, Churchill initially supported the highly integrated European Defence Community plan because he could understand France's reasons for wanting to control any German rearmament so soon after the war within the framework of some military equivalent to the Coal and Steel Community formed in 1950.

The issue became more urgent as the Cold War worsened, but in August 1954 a hostile vote in the French National Assembly destroyed the Defence Community model. Churchill worked hard to be fair to both France and West Germany and fully supported the patient shuttle diplomacy of his Foreign Secretary. In 1955, Eden secured a historic agreement with France to the rearming of West Germany within NATO – provided it renounced any right to nuclear weapons. Adenauer was always fearful of the major powers using Germany as a bargaining counter to de-fuse Cold War tensions, but the tone and substance of Churchill's interventions in this crisis were a vital reassurance to him.

The mounting dangers of the Cold War and of an atomic and nuclear arms race became Churchill's greatest preoccupation in the time that remained to him as Prime Minister. He continued to believe in the value of personal summit diplomacy and of talking directly to Stalin and then, after 1953, his successors. His advisers, especially in the Foreign Office, while marvelling at the tenacious optimism of a Prime Minister nearing his eightieth birthday, feared the unease it injected into relations between Britain and the Eisenhower administration which took office at the start of 1952. Churchill held his ground, telling RA

Butler, his Chancellor of the Exchequer over dinner in March 1954 that talks with the Russians to halt the arms race were 'the only political interest he had left.'

Two visits by Churchill to Eisenhower failed to convince the President. Returning by sea from the second trip in carly July 1954, Churchill caused a real crisis, not only in relations with Washington but with his own Cabinet, when on his own initiative he sent a telegram to Molotov, the Soviet Foreign Minister, suggesting they meet without American participation. Some of Churchill's ministers considered resignation over this. Molotov replied discreetly, welcoming talks but stressing the importance of American

left: Chartwell.

above: Plaque at Chartwell. After the war the house had not been
lived in for years and fewer staff could be afforded. A group of admirers
gathered together and bought the house for Churchill, presenting
it to the National Trust.

inclusion and Churchill survived the anger of colleagues, telling the Cabinet that his action was a product of his 'anxiety to lose no opportunity of furthering the cause of world peace.' He also wrote, in similar but rather more contrite terms, to Eisenhower, who answered him that their relationship remained intact but added that 'personal trust based upon more than a dozen years of close association and valued friendship may occasionally permit room for amazement but never suspicion.'

In the midst of this drama Churchill put to the Cabinet the case for a British nuclear weapon to be built and tested, yet his efforts to further the cause of peace by direct contacts with the Soviet leaders were genuine.

Was he ahead of his time in working to bring about what finally happened after Mikhail Gorbachev took power in 1985? Some historians now think so and perhaps as the end of his political life approached he really did want to enter history as a peacemaker. On 1 March 1955, in his last major Prime Ministerial speech to Parliament he returned to his theme of how no superpower could hide from the awful might of nuclear weapons, while stressing eloquently the continuing case for personal diplomacy as a way of controlling events. 'Mercifully,' he told a hushed chamber, 'there is time and hope if we combine patience and courage', and he ended: 'The day may dawn when fair play, love for one's fellow men, respect for justice and freedom, will enable generations to march forth serene and triumphant from the hideous epoch in which we have to dwell. Meanwhile never flinch, never weary, never despair.'

'Never Despair' is the title Sir Martin Gilbert chose for the eighth and final volume of his monumental official life of Churchill. In it he covers fully Churchill's international role after 1945 but also does full justice to the work of his second administration on the domestic front after 1951. The election of October that year was a bitter one, with Churchill taking legal action against the Daily Mirror after it accused him of being a warmonger. Labour argued that its welfare legislation would be at risk under a change of government but Churchill, back in power, held spending on the Health Service to a level identical with what it had been since its inception in 1948.

'Set the people free' had been an election slogan cheerfully supported by him in 1951 and his ministers did indeed carry out a bonfire of wartime controls and regulations. Labour had in fact already started this process but of the industries it had brought into public ownership, only iron and steel production and road haulage were returned to private hands. Churchill insisted, too, that his ministers work in close consultation with the trade unions and not until 1955 did the level of strikes even begin to edge above that for any single year between 1946 and 1951.

After October 1951, when his party had, after all, returned to power with a smaller share than Labour of the total vote cast, Churchill led as a moderate and demanded moderation from his colleagues. This has been called 'the Conservative compromise' of the 1950s and in his autumnal years, Churchill would have accepted the description. It does, after all, invest with a certain symmetry the political career which Churchill had embarked upon half a century before as a moderate social reformer.

right: The statue of Churchill opposite the Houses of Parliament.

By 1955, Sir Anthony Eden was becoming frustrated at his long wait for the succession. Though he never challenged his leader openly, he was not averse to stressing, in his contacts with Washington, that some of the Prime Minister's very personal initiatives like the Molotov telegram could be attributed to increasing senility. This is very doubtful, since Churchill's belief in the need for talks with the Soviet leadership was perfectly genuine.

He had however, passed his eightieth birthday by then and the rigours of a long and punishing public life were catching up on him. He had suffered a minor stroke while on holiday in France in 1949, and, in June 1953, had a much more serious one which incapacitated him until August. Amazingly as it would seem now, the media observed total silence about this, despite widespread rumours, and he recovered enough to address the Conservative Conference in October and to resume his work in Downing Street.

He finally tendered his resignation to the new Queen on 5 April 1955, having declined all titles other than a knighthood in her Coronation year. Ten years remained for him to live, or latterly merely to endure, as his health deteriorated. For a time he occupied himself by revising for publication his *History of the English Speaking Peoples* and he travelled, painted and read as well as finding solace in music and the simple pleasures of home life at Chartwell.

Lady Mary Soames, when she wrote much later of her father's twilight years, recalled lines written by the poet Walter Savage Landor: 'I warmed both hands before the fire of life, it sinks and I am ready to depart.' Churchill died on 24 January 1965.

Six days later, great crowds watched as his coffin was carried through the London streets by slow-marching troops to St Paul's Cathedral. It was then taken up the Thames for burial at Bladon in Oxfordshire, close to his birthplace.

Churchill had been born into a Victorian and high imperial age, but an imperial Britain slipped out of history with Churchill's funeral cortege on Saturday, 30 January, 1965, as a very different multicultural society began to emerge. Its people were starting to set aside illusions about a great global role for Britain and some of them perhaps subscribed to the view of Jimmy Porter, anti-hero of John Osborne's 1956 play, *Look Back in Anger* that there were no brave causes left. Yet, at the time of Churchill's death, Britain's defiance of Hitler seemed such a cause and still does to freedom loving people here and in many other countries. Defeat in 1940, surrender, or a compromise peace would have made certain long years of evil tyranny over much of Europe. It would then have fallen to the Soviet Union, with all its own cruel short-comings, to decide whether to challenge Hitler, but it would have been as hard for it to attempt that without an ally in Europe, as it would have been for the United States to do so, without a secure base on the British Isles. Both powers were influenced by Britain's will to fight on, a will driven and personified by Churchill. As a result, the course of 20th century history was altered decidedly for the better.

overleaf: **Churchill's State Funeral.**
The cortége is shown having passed the Cenotaph, in Whitehall, London.